ETERNALLY YOURS

For Velda and Leon —
Looking forward to
our 60th Anniversary —
Don't forget to spend
your kisses! Denny Smith
12/20/96

Dau Smith

Jack Smith
ETERNALLY YOURS

A collection of columns

by the late Los Angeles Times writer

compiled by his wife DENISE SMITH

and his sons CURT and DOUG

Los Angeles Times

1996

Los Angeles Times

Editor: Carla Lazzareschi
Book Design and Typography: Michael Diehl

Library of Congress Catalog Card Number: 96-78401

Smith, Jack Clifford, 1916–1996
Eternally Yours

ISBN 0-9653061-0-0

Published by the Los Angeles Times
Times Mirror Square, Los Angeles, California 90053
A Times Mirror Company

First printing October 1996

Printed in the U.S.A.

Table of Contents

To all of Jack's readers—

Those who simply appreciated his column,
those whose responses generated more columns,
and even those who, as Jack put it,
"circle around like vultures waiting to swoop"
when he made one of his infamous "two mistakes a year."
Our thanks for giving him the incentive
to keep writing until the very end.

— Denny, Curt and Doug

Introduction

THIS IS A COLLECTION of columns representing Jack's views on life, his family and the remarkable century he lived in. A few of the selections come from his earlier works, but generally we've tried to capture the perspective of a professional journalist working 15 years beyond retirement age and up to the last days of his life. Inevitably, the work of Jack's last 10 years focused on the only topic that a man in his declining condition could with first-hand observation: his own death. Although some readers found his health inventories tedious and self-pitying, many more were both warmed by his placid observations of the pains and indignities of old age and encouraged by his recounting of the new feelings and consolations of his journey.

As a columnist, Jack was fundamentally an observer, a chronicler of the vagaries of his own family and the larger family of mankind. It seemed he always had a deadline: for 12 years, three columns a week while working full time as a rewrite man at the Los Angeles Times; another 21 years as a full-time, five-days-a-week columnist; finally retiring in 1992 to one column a week.

For that reason, he sometimes seemed remote, detached. He lived and slept with the specter of that deadline, which is what he passionately chose to do. It was always in the back of his mind, even when he was enjoying the company of his family and his friends or spending an evening at the theater or the Philharmonic or at Dodger Stadium. When he had only the seed of an idea, it had to germinate and slowly develop in his consciousness until he could bring it forth in full flower as a column.

The search for the meaning of life and man's place in it was a theme that periodically showed up in Jack's columns. He pursued the answer in a secular way and synthesized the answer into a phrase that showed up in various forms over a period of years. When he said, "The purpose of life is to keep on living and see what happens next," that was, perhaps, the essence of his philosophy.

Beyond saying this, we are reluctant to explain what this book is about. We've tried to make it about everything that came under Jack's curious gaze, from love and war to the eternal meaning in the plight of a bee caught in a spider's web. Yet we know it's more than a collection of random and passing thoughts. Its message, as we read it, is that one can bear the worst of illness and decrepitude without ever losing one's love of life and one's purpose within a family.

■　　■　　■

The Smith family thanks The Los Angeles Times for helping us perpetuate Jack's spirit with this book; Carla Lazzareschi, associate editor of Times on Demand, for conceiving the project and unflaggingly seeing it through, giving us guidance in the selection and arrangement of the columns; and Jean Wudke, for years the anonymous voice behind Jack's playful and clever headlines, for coming out of retirement to do it again.

CHAPTER 1

In the Beginning

Jack Smith: He Just Doesn't Look Like a Quentin Randolph

Sunday, February 17, 1985

I USED TO SPEND hours in my youth imagining romantic names for myself, names that evoked my character, or the character I hoped to have: Quentin Randolph, Fulton Duffield, Marshall Kent, Lancelot Grant, Morgan Cortright. I would write them down and roll them about on my tongue.

Jack Smith is something of an embarrassment, being the most common name in the English-speaking world. I actually don't mind its being common, since I have no pretensions; but I do mind being accused of having made it up to conceal my true identity—as if I had no more imagination than that.

How often in my younger years, when I registered at a hotel with my wife, did I notice the slight smirk of conspiracy on the face of the registration clerk, which somehow was transmitted to the bellman, who wore it up in the elevator, and, naturally, expected a larger tip, since he also was conniving at an illicit adventure.

What always ired me on these occasions was not the implicit suggestion that I was engaged in a sinful enterprise, but that I was such a dolt that I couldn't think up a better phony name for myself than Jack Smith.

Fortunately, this contretemps rarely occurs anymore, because the young don't think that a man my age could be committing a sin, and also because on checking in one is required to show the universal identification—a plastic credit card.

I don't know how I managed to get married with a name

like Jack Smith. My wife's name, when I met her, was Denise Bresson, which was exotic enough. She didn't know it at the time, but it had once been Dusserre-Bresson; but her grandfather had dropped the Dusserre.

When I was in school it was common for love-struck girls to spend their classroom time writing the names of their *inamorata* over and over in their notebooks, prefacing the unsuspecting lad's name with the magic *Mrs.* I just don't think a romantic young schoolgirl—for that is what she was—could have made the jump all the way from Denise Dusserre-Bresson to Mrs. Jack Smith. Without the hyphenation it must not have been so hard. In any case, she did it.

I had a chance to change my name when I first began writing this column—26 years years ago. Washington Irving Ramsdell, then editor of the editorial pages, who got me started, and a man, obviously, who appreciated a name of literary resonance, asked me what name I wanted to write under. I was already writing as a reporter under the name Jack Smith.

I was thrown into a maelstrom of possibilities. Here was a chance, at last, to reshape my image, my persona, perhaps my life. What would it be? Quentin Randolph? Fulton Duffield? Morgan Cortright? Any one of them would give me the luster I wanted. They exuded dignity, schooling, tradition; they would speak of famous soldiers in my background; of poets and great lovers and statesmen, and perhaps a famous Shakespearean actor or two.

And certainly a name like Quentin Randolph would add weight to anything I wrote.

But in the end I couldn't do it.

I thought of my father, who had borne Smith proudly all his life; and of his father and all the Smiths before him. I thought of all the Smiths who had labored honorably at their anvils through the centuries to bring man out of the Stone

Age. We Smiths were, after all, the forge upon which civilization had been shaped, and we were the shapers.

Besides, I was afraid that sooner or later, in a bar someplace, or at a social, I would encounter someone who had known me at school, or in the Civilian Conservation Corps, or in the Marines, and who would inevitably blurt it out:

"Why, son of a gun, if it isn't old Jack Smith!"

Most of all, I worried that if I called myself Quentin Randolph, I would begin trying to think like a Quentin Randolph, and I didn't know how a Quentin Randolph thought.

So I stayed Jack Smith; and what you see is what you get.

Pitching the Star Spangled Banter

Thursday, February 7, 1985

MAN'S VAINEST YEARNING is his wish to be remembered long after he is gone; to leave behind him on Earth some marker that will remind his descendants, into eternity, that he passed this way.

Actually, most of us can't expect to be remembered beyond the third or fourth generation; and not even then, unless we are especially good, and leave a lot of land and money; or especially bad, and become a legend.

But the yearning cannot be repressed. That's why graveyards prosper, and there will always be tombstone cutters.

The record of man's presence on Earth is so brief—only a few thousand years—that we still have the illusion that our heroes will be remembered for all time; that they will remain forever in the human consciousness through the monuments erected in their honor.

Thus, we will never forget the brooding Lincoln of the Memorial; the victorious Nelson of Trafalgar Square; the serene Ramses the Great, contemplating the known world from his four colossal statues at Abu Simbel; the imperial Marcus Aurelius, forever mounted on his bronze steed in Michelangelo's piazza; and, carved for the ages in the granite of Mt. Rushmore, the faces of Washington, Jefferson, Lincoln and Teddy Roosevelt.

But, alas, the faces of Mt. Rushmore will be worn away, too, one day, even as the mountains themselves are leveled by the tears of time. Trafalgar Square will someday be dug up by archeologists who will come upon the vain little man in the admiral's hat and say, "And who was this funny fellow?"; our brooding Lincoln will be pulverized, perhaps in the first intercontinental nuclear mistake; Ramses in time will surrender to the encroaching freeze of the nuclear night; and the Rome of Marcus Aurelius will lie nine cities down, like Troy.

How, then, are we to leave our mark, never to be forgotten?

A reader, Robert B. Inkelas of Santa Monica, thinks he has found the answer. He has sent me a little leaflet advertising "The Gift That Lasts Forever."

For $35—send your money in with the ad, get a $5 discount—you can have a star—a real star—named for you or for anyone else you name.

I had heard a few pitches for this new scheme on my car radio, but had never seen it in writing before. Here it is:

"Imagine the unending Cosmos, linked for eternity with someone you love. Now, honor your children, parents, or that special person by having the International Star Registry name a real star after them. The name you select will be permanently recorded in the Copyright Office of the Library of Congress, and in the Registry's vaults in Switzerland.

"The recipient of your unique gift will receive a 12" by 16" hand-inscribed parchment, two sky charts, and actual tele-scope coordinates for locating their star in the night sky. All sent in a sturdy gift box along with the booklet 'Our Place in the Cosmos....'

"Follow in the footsteps of great people who already have their place in the stars: Harry James, Andy Williams, Frank Sinatra and Bette Davis are among the many...."

At first glance it's a staggering idea.

Imagine looking out into the black night and seeing a distant star blinking at you and being able to say, "That's my star—that's Jack Smith!"

It might seem funny calling a star anything as plain as Jack Smith, compared with Alpha Centauri, Sirius, Groombridge, Epsilon Indi, and even, for that matter, Frank Sinatra.

Just imagine, having a star with your name burning out there in space, forever, twinkling out your message to the Earth: *Jack Smith was here!*

But it's hard to imagine there being very many of anything as big as stars. Don't worry. Carl Sagan tells us, in "Cosmos," that there are more stars in the cosmos than there are grains of sand on all the beaches of the world. At least.

A galaxy is composed of billions upon billions of stars; our own galaxy, our Milky Way, has about 100 billion; and there are some 100 billion galaxies. So there are plenty of stars to go around, although you can't expect to *see* your own star.

But what about permanence? Will it hang out up there for you forever, a great glowing ball of hydrogen and helium, burning at 40 million degrees at its core throughout eternity? No, alas; in time even the brightest star will burn itself out from all this constant internal combustion and radiation, and collapse inward into a hard hot mass called a white dwarf, or worse, a black hole.

In its death throes, even our sun, like other stars, will flare out into a red giant, engulfing the nearer planets and perhaps even the Earth—at last melting our icecaps, boiling our oceans and roasting us all, together with our little houses, institutions and monuments.

So even the stars are doomed; and there isn't much point in having one named for you if it's just going to burn out on you.

Anyway, International Star Registry has been discredited by astronomers, who say that only the International Astronomical Union can name stars, and that people who pay for having a star named after them might as well throw their money into a black hole, which is nothing but a very dead, very dense star.

I think what I'll do, for my own immortality, is go down to our house in Baja and go down to the beach and find a likely looking grain of sand, and name it Jack Smith, and throw it back in.

Heaven: Nothing to Write Home About

Monday, December 12, 1994

THERE HAS BEEN much talk lately about heaven.

There is much testimony that it does not exist. For heaven's sake what would we do without it? The language would be sadly weakened were there no mild expletives such as those derived from the word itself.

Little boys and girls are taught not to say, "The hell with it," though I can't see why. Many times when I was a small boy I felt like saying it and sometimes did. But they can say "for heaven's sake" or "thank heaven" or any other variation of that celestial nowhere.

I used to think the word was especially favored by older women. Whenever she was taken by mild surprise, my grandmother used to say, "Heavens to Betsy," though she never gave us a clue as to who Betsy might be. Of course to suggest that such locutions are the province of older women is sexist and ageist. I don't want to do that. Heavens to Betsy!

Heaven is not only thought of in our culture as a nice place to live but also as a source of power or benign favor, like God himself.

The language is replete with such supplications as "Heaven help us!" and "Heaven will help the working girl." The latter evidently derives from the early 20th Century when young women first entered the work force and were oppressed and harassed by their male associates. Heaven help them, indeed.

Evidently there is a flood of recent books about heaven, some of them by people who have been there. I do not believe a dead person, or a person who has been dead, can write a book (though I have read some that read like it).

Heaven is thought to be a place of eternal bliss. For whom? One can hardly imagine a place that would be bliss for everyone. Eternal bliss is eternal boredom. Imagine lying on a bed of pansies on a nice spring day under a peach tree while naked maidens dance all about. Soon one would want to turn on the TV or read the comic page.

What if heaven were an eternal replay of the USC-UCLA football game? Is there anything that one would want to see over and over again, no matter who won?

No. It seems to me impossible for anyone to write a script for a perfect day in heaven. For one thing, what is life without conflict? Even life without defeat? What if USC always won? Worse yet, what if they always tied—as they did last month? Heaven would theoretically have to be an eternal tie. What a bore.

In heaven (one supposes), everything would be suffused in soft lights and soft music. OK. But what about those who wanted to read the newspaper? What about those who wanted to hear hard rock? (I assume in all fairness a few of them would get in.)

Surely there would be no politics in heaven. Would a citizen like to wake up and read (if there was enough light) that the government had been overturned in a military coup? Who, even in hell, wants that?

I have never been dead, but I think I have been close enough to know what it's like. I was in a coma once a few years ago. My heart had stopped. All signs of life had vanished. The doctor told my wife not to expect me to live. I had been on the other shore. Believe me, there was nothing there. No light. No music. No perfume. No football game.

There is no law (this is a democracy, remember) against a person saying that he or she has been to heaven. But they'd better bring home some pictures or I'm not going to believe them.

I see no reason to believe that in case of my death I would not be admitted to heaven. Oh, I've committed a few sins, but nothing felonious. I don't know what the rules of admission are, but if half of us get there the place is going to be as overcrowded as hell. It will be as cosmopolitan as Los Angeles and twice as hectic. Half of us will be USC fans and half UCLA. We will have the same amount of conflict as we do here and the same amounts of joy and misery.

Nobody knows where heaven is. Jesus is said to have ascended to heaven, which suggests that it's up. But space is all around us. He could just as well have descended.

No planet is big enough to hold the dead of all time. So heaven must just hang free, out there in space. But then there wouldn't be any gravity. You couldn't even play Ping-Pong.

My advice to anyone is that if they come for you, don't go.

Wanna Be 100? Lie About Your Age

Monday, June 17, 1985

"EVERY DAY 30 Americans turn 100," the letter began. "Will you be one of them?"

Since I haven't the slightest chance or hope of turning 100, it wasn't a very provocative question.

However, granting that I might not become a centenarian, the letter offered to show how I could find out whether I might exceed my own life expectancy, as calculated by actuaries, or fall short of it.

A questionnaire, prepared by Cadwell Davis Partners, advertising, was enclosed.

"The average life expectancy for a person of your age and sex has been calculated by actuaries. However, you can add months, years, even decades to your life, or foreshorten it, depending upon your family life, personality, fitness, work, play, health and heredity. No matter what your age, you'll see opportunities to prolong your life by changing a few habits."

The test included a number of questions, the answers to which would indicate whether you could add anywhere from three months to two years to your life expectancy, or had to deduct so many months from it.

For example, if you are single and over 40, you have to deduct six months. If you are a widow or a widower you have to deduct six months. If your home life is extremely pleasant and calm you *add* six months.

Being neither single nor divorced, and having an extremely calm and pleasant home life, most of the time, I added six months to my life expectancy, which is, given my age and sex, 79 years.

That meant, to start with, that having an extremely pleasant and calm home life, I could expect to live to 79 years and six months.

So far so good. But almost immediately I lost that extra six months. The question was: Are you tense and nervous most of the time? If so, deduct six months.

So I'm back to 79.

Then I lost six months by being a Type A personality—very competitive, always rushed, do many things at once.

I lost another six months for living in a city. (If you live in a small town or on a farm you can add three months.)

If you're satisfied with your sexual activity you can add nine months; but if you aren't satisfied, you don't have to deduct anything.

Evidently that means that not being satisfied with your sex life won't reduce your life expectancy any. As for my own sex life, I have always considered that a private matter.

If you get 20 or 30 minutes of vigorous exercise at least three times a week you can add 12 months. I have just recently started exercising at the Pasadena Athletic Club, riding a bicycle for 20 minutes, while I watch the "Today" show, then working the rowing machine for 20 minutes.

The good of this program may be undone, however, by my habit of rewarding myself for exercising by going to the Konditori for breakfast after every session, and having a hamburger with one egg, over easy.

However, if my exercise counts, I am two years ahead of anyone who doesn't exercise. They have to *deduct* 12 months.

I get three months for drinking low-fat milk only, and

three months for eating high-fiber foods. For not smoking I can add six months. (Moderate smoking takes off 12 months and heavy smoking 24.)

Since I drink alcohol in what I consider moderation I have to deduct six months. If I drank never or seldom I could add six months.

The question seems to be this: Assuming that my life expectancy is 79, do I want to give up drinking merely to be able to live another six months at the end? Right now, I don't think so. Maybe when I'm 79 I'll feel different.

I get to add three months, though, because my job satisfaction is above average. (Though I don't know what average job satisfaction is.)

If you take a vacation at least once a year you can add six months. I don't know how to answer that. I have taken some vacations, in my leaner days, on which I got another job and worked. Last year I didn't take a vacation at all. I wonder whether, if I take a vacation this year, I'll get my six extra months.

If you're regularly exposed to air pollution you have to deduct three months; if you're regularly exposed in substantial amounts, deduct nine months. Since I live close to downtown Los Angeles I suppose I am regularly exposed; but whether that exposure is substantial, I don't know. I'm splitting it and taking six months off my life.

I haven't listed all the factors that are said to effect either a longer or shorter life span. However, if my addition is accurate, there is no way *anyone* can get to be 100, so the original question is a fraud, it seems to me.

I added up all the possible plus factors and got only 93 months—so if I could count them all, with *no* deductions for minus factors, I would still outlive my life expectancy only by seven years and nine months.

My true score shows that I'm going to have only six extra months.

So how do you get to be a centenarian?

I have an idea you get to be a centenarian by having grandparents with good genes; you drink a little, smoke a little, make love a little, and, like Hank Williams, you "Don't worry 'bout nothin', 'cause nothin' ain't gonna work out all right nohow."

Here Lies...in 50 Words or Less

Wednesday, October 31, 1990

MY COLLEAGUE Nardi Reeder Campion, who writes a column, "Everyday Matters," that is widely read on the East Coast, sends me one describing a parlor game she calls "Write Your Own Epitaph."

"You write down, in 50 words or less, what you would like to have on your tombstone. Then the leader reads the epitaphs aloud and the players have to guess who wrote them."

Epitaphs are fun, and sometimes very revealing. I applaud the 50-word limit, since brevity is the soul of epitaphs, as well as of wit. Campion recalls the tombstone for a wife that said simply:

I told you I was sick.

That is in the genre of "the last word" epitaphs.

Campion also quotes one from the old Jaffrey, N.H., cemetery, near her home:

Sarah Averill

89 years, 5 months, 5 days

She done all she could

As Campion says, "None of us could ask for more."

Considering his many achievements, Benjamin Franklin's epitaph was extremely modest. His stone bears only four words and a date:

Benjamin and Deborah Franklin

1790

Coincidentally, Fallon Evans, a professor of English, writes from Cambridge, England, where he is teaching a group from the Los Angeles Community Colleges this semester, about the language of an epitaph he found in a Victorian graveyard there.

Affectionate Remembrance

of JOHN TAYLOR

Who departed this life Dec. 1, 1878

Aged 56

Goodbye dear wife and children all

I bid this world adieu

My troubles on this world were great

My pleasures few,

Also Charlotte, wife of the above

Who died Feb. 2, 1900,

Aged 82 yrs

"My complaint," Evans says, "is about their use of the English language; one would think that they would have got the hang of it here, but no." What he objects to is the word *above*. In fact, he argues, Taylor lies below, not above. I would say that depends on whether one is thinking of his bones or of his soul.

In a compendium of articles from Vanity Fair of the 1920s and 1930s I find two pages of epitaphs written for themselves by celebrities of those times.

Some are elegantly brief:

Here Lies

Michael Arlen

As usual

George S. Kaufman seemed to think of himself as below.

His epitaph:

Over my dead body

The Marx Brothers concocted an epitaph for all four of them:

Here lie the
Four Marx Brothers
The first time they ever went out as a team

Zoe Akins simply listed the things she loved:

She loved
Shakespeare's sonnets
Paris bonnets.
Country walks,
All-night talks,
Old trees and places
Children's faces
Shaw and Keats,
Opera seats,
Lonely prairies,
Tea at Sherry's,
Sunlight and air,
Vanity Fair

Dorothy Parker's was brief and sassy, like almost everything she wrote:

Excuse my dust!

Wallace Irwin indulged in a flight of self-congratulation:

Here lies Wallace Irwin of genius
so bright
He flashed like a sun where there
might have been night;
Poet, philosopher, novelist, sage,
O! What adornments he lent to his age!
Gifts such as his cannot wither and die,
Though he has joined the immortals on high,

For his works glow like pearls on a Seven-foot shelf.
(Note, by the sexton: "He wrote this himself.")

Alas, his flash has faded. I had to look him up in Benet's Reader's Encyclopedia. Wallace Irwin (1875-1959), it says, was a newspaperman and writer of humorous verse and fiction. He won national fame with "Love Sonnets of a Hoodlum." *Sic transit gloria mundi.*

Perhaps the only epitaph among these that is still quoted (except for "Excuse my dust!") is the one W. C. Fields wrote for himself:

Here lies
W. C. Fields
I'd rather be living in Philadelphia

Fields was born in Philadelphia, a city that he heartily disparaged in later life. His epitaph is often misquoted as "All things considered, I'd rather be living in Philadelphia."

Like most epitaphs written in life, it did not survive him. His tomb in Forest Lawn bears only the simple inscription "W. C. Fields, 1880-1946."

Ben Franklin's epitaph too was not the one he had written for himself. It is inscribed in Ben's script on copper at the Yale University Library, and reads:

The body of
B. Franklin, printer;
Like the cover of an old book,
Its contents torn out,
And stript of its lettering and gilding,
Lies here, food for worms.
But the work shall not be wholly lost:
For it will, as he believ'd, appear once more
In a new & more perfect edition,
corrected and amended
By the author.

Though I doubt that it will ever grace my tombstone, I offer as my epitaph the following:

Have a nice day

CHAPTER 2

A Close Call

Following Steve Can Be a Pain in the *What?*

Reprinted from Alive In La La Land, 1989

A T   F I R S T   I wasn't alarmed. I was merely puzzled. It wasn't a pain in my chest. A pain in the chest was angina. The classic symptom of heart trouble.

It was more of an ache. It was in my back and shoulders. It came and went. It was just a low-grade ache, not especially painful. It was like the ache you get when you have thrown a ball too hard or made an awkward reach backward. In a moment it would go away.

Then I began to notice other symptoms. Sometimes the ache would be accompanied by a feeling of fatigue. Sometimes I perspired and felt faint.

I began to associate the trouble with certain activities, looking for some telltale relationship. I noticed that the ache often came when I was under stress.

I was often under stress at that time. I was not only writing five columns a week for the Los Angeles Times but also making talks around Southern California to library support groups, to journalism groups, and simply here and there, whenever I was called on.

One night when I was to make a talk before the Friends of the La Verne Library, my wife and I had dinner earlier at the home of one of the friends. It was warm and pleasant, and I enjoyed the company and the meal.

We drove to the university, where I was to talk at Founders Hall. We parked the car across the street and got out. It was rather chilly for Southern California. As we walked across the street, I began to feel faint. Once inside the hall, I said, "I think I'd better sit down for a minute."

I sat in a wooden chair in the entrance hall. My shoulders began to ache. Perspiration broke out on my forehead. I trembled. I wondered whether I was having a heart attack or what I should do.

Suddenly the symptoms went away. Strength flowed back into me. I was all right. Whatever it was, it wasn't important.

I got up and went into the auditorium and talked the usual 45 minutes.

A week or two later I attended an awards ceremony in Hollywood. I was receiving an award for some Hollywood women's advertising group on one pretext or another. So was Steve Allen. For some inexplicable reason Allen was called on to speak before I was.

I sat there at my table realizing that I was going to have to follow Steve Allen. It was not an enviable position. I felt a streak of pain in my upper arms and across my shoulders. I began to perspire. I felt faint.

Whatever it was, then, it was definitely associated with stress.

I decided it was time to tell my doctor about it. I described the symptoms and the circumstances in which they appeared.

He shook his head skeptically. "I doubt if it's got anything to do with your heart," he said. "There's just nothing in your history to indicate heart trouble."

It was true. By outward appearance I did not look like a prime prospect for a heart attack. I was 67 years old, but I had always been thin. My blood pressure was under control. I wasn't a weekend athlete. I didn't exert myself. I didn't smoke.

Actually, I hadn't worried much about my heart. In his classic book, "Type A Behavior and Your Heart," Dr. Meyer Friedman's first paragraph had been a quotation from my column in The Times:

"Sometime ago," I had written, "I quit worrying about what to do, or not to do, to keep from having a heart attack. I was so confused by all the conflicting theories that I began developing the symptoms."

My doctor told me to let him know if my pain recurred.

I Flunked the Angiogram

Reprinted from Alive In La La Land, 1989

A week or so later I was walking up a ramp with my wife to buy tickets for a trip to Catalina when the pain came suddenly and hard. It was deep and lasting. I had to sit down until it went away.

I went back to my doctor. That was enough for him.

"We'll have to give you a stress test," he said.

He made an appointment for me at Huntington Memorial Hospital, and I went in for my stress test. A stress test consists mainly of walking on a treadmill at a gradually increasing speed and degree of incline. Meanwhile, your blood pressure and your heart rate are monitored.

After three minutes I was unable to go on.

I had flunked the test.

My doctor said it was time to consult a cardiologist.

The cardiologist was a pleasant, polite, low-key Southern gentlemen who seemed unflappable. He said I would have to have an angiogram.

The angiogram is a supposedly simple procedure in which a plastic catheter is inserted into an artery in the thigh, threaded through the body and into the aorta itself. Dyes are passed through the catheter and photographed by X-ray. If the blood vessels that send blood to the heart are blocked by fatty tissues, as in atherosclerosis, the flow of dye is shut off or squeezed down to a trickle.

One must stay in the hospital overnight for an angiogram. It is, I have since learned, a rather hazardous procedure. But it is not entirely unpleasant. One is lightly drugged, and one can lie back and watch the dye enter one's heart on a screen.

I flunked the angiogram, too.

"What does that mean?" I asked my cardiologist.

He said it meant surgery. I would have to have a coronary bypass.

Bypass is medical vernacular for coronary artery bypass graft surgery—in which the surgeon takes a length of vein from one's leg and grafts it from the aorta to the heart, bypassing a blocked coronary artery.

It was merely a phrase to me. Some of my friends had had them. They all swore it was a piece of cake. They felt better afterward than they had in 10 years.

The operation has become so commonplace as to seem trivial, but it is still a major operation.

My cardiologist called in the surgeon, who, of course, corroborated his finding.

I didn't argue. I didn't demand a second opinion. I believed I was in good hands.

"When do you want to do it?" I asked.

"Tuesday," the surgeon said.

That was Friday.

Zeroing In on Him Again

Reprinted from Alive In La La Land, 1989

N O   M A T T E R how routine heart surgery has become, there is always a chance that the patient will die.

I didn't give a lot of thought to it. I had committed my share of sins in my life; I would like to have been able to undo them—at least some of them; but when the bell tolls, you don't get a second chance.

Or do you?

I had faced death at least once before. I had landed in the third wave with the Marines on Iwo Jima, an island whose name, sad to say, means nothing to the youth of today.

The Japanese were shelling the beach ferociously. At the time our amtrac landed, casualties were running 75%. The chances for survival were not good. I ran up the beach and stumbled down into a shell hole made either by a Japanese field piece or by our own preparatory naval gunfire. Two other men clambered into the hole behind me. We could hardly talk above the din.

We looked at each other dumbly. Fear was the common denominator. I suggested that we should get out of the hole, because if we stayed there it would soon take another hit. The Japanese were zeroed in on that beach.

"We have to get off the beach and go on forward," I argued. I was a sergeant, but not a line sergeant. I had no authority over those marines. I have often wondered since whether they saw the No. 3 on the back of my blouse, for sergeant, and deferred to my rank.

They agreed, and the two of them climbed up to the lip of

the hole and flung themselves forward, over the top. I was right behind them. Just as my head reached the top of the hole, a shell landed a few feet forward of it. My helmet rang as if hit by a sledgehammer. I was stunned. When my head cleared, I climbed on up and out of the hole.

One of my comrades had vanished. The other was in a kneeling position, as if praying. He had no head.

Besides carrying a lifelong load of guilt over that incident, I have always wondered why I was spared.

I thought of myself as having had a second chance.

Now, with most of my life spent and few of my sins expiated, I was about to have heart surgery, and if I was lucky, I would have yet another chance.

If I survived, would it make any difference in my life? Would I live more fully? Would I be more generous, kind, loving?

I checked into the hospital on Tuesday, and on Wednesday morning they wheeled me into surgery. I was so drugged that philosophical introspections were beyond me. Deep down, I knew that I might never wake up, but it didn't really trouble me.

I was in surgery four and a half hours. My surgeon did four bypasses, not one; on the table I suffered a minor heart attack, and one of the bypasses did not work.

I am not going to describe the operation step by step. I never asked about it, for one thing. Also, I don't share the common notion that everyone is interested in everyone else's operation.

Looking back, I'm sure that the most disturbing part of the entire experience was my loss of mental stability during my recovery.

I am increasingly aware of my faults and weaknesses, but until then I was satisfied that in a mad world I was relatively sane. In every crisis, no matter how poorly I may have acted out of character deficiency, I at least knew what was what.

A Rousing Welcome

Reprinted from Alive In La La Land, 1989

Something unexpected and wonderful waited for us the day my wife drove me up the hill to our house after my two weeks in the hospital.

Our house is on the corner of the top of a steep rise, so that you come upon it suddenly. My surprise was complete.

It was a white paper poster—2 feet high and 14 feet long—with this message blocked in across it in green crayon:

WELCOME HOME
WE LOVE YOU, MR. SMITH

It was supported by two poles planted among my wife's African daisies, and no one who drove up the hill could miss it.

Up close, we saw that it was signed by Eric and Sarah and April and Elaine and Tanya and Gabriel and Karen and Michael and Amy and Nicole and Robert and Christopher and Carlos and dozens of other children who go to the little Mt. Washington School at the top of the hill.

Our own boys had gone through the school, and my wife had been president of the PTA. It has always had an exuberant spirit, and I have often gone up for a visit, in recent years, just to cheer myself up and restore my faith in schools, teachers, and children. Now they had brought their cheer to me.

I tottered up the steps to our door on my wife's arm and stood there gasping, reminded painfully of my devastating weakness. At the same time I was laughing. The poster had made me laugh, because men don't cry.

My cardiologist, who speaks with a gentle Southern inflection that seems to make even bad news sound rather pleasant, had warned me that patients were often depressed after heart surgery.

"Why is that?" I asked. I may be disenchanted, but I remain buoyant, and I have always thought of depression as something ridiculous that you simply get, like gallstones.

The patient is depressed, the doctor told me, because he is obliged to contemplate his own mortality. I assured him that the certainty of mortality was an old acquaintance of mine and I would have no trouble with it.

I was depressed for weeks. But I don't think my heart was as much the cause of it as my nose. Evidently in yanking out my oxygen tube in the intensive care unit I had damaged the mucous membrane and had come home with a stubborn infection that filled my nose with crust, blocking the passages and making it hard or impossible for me to breathe in a normal way. The usual remedies failed or made it worse; finally, I went to an ear, nose, and throat man who gave me temporary relief by cleaning out my nose with tweezers, made laboratory tests of the infection, and prescribed a penicillin drug that eventually made me well.

I don't want to depress the reader with tedious medical details, but I describe this affliction to help explain, perhaps, my curious mental incapacity during this period.

As many patients secretly do, I suspect, I had looked forward to my convalescence. There would be a time, I imagined, when I would be over the shock and pain and before I was fit enough to go back to work, when the days would seem idyllic. Only lightly drugged, excused from every responsibility, I could read, watch TV, putter about, write thank-you notes, gradually begin to reconnect, every now and then reminding myself, I don't *have* to do anything.

I enjoyed no such interlude. The combination of physical frailty and difficulty in breathing kept me in a state of unrelieved anxiety. I couldn't concentrate. I kept trying things and bumping into my limits. I couldn't sleep. Every time I was about to drop off I remembered that I couldn't breathe through my nose. I worried that I would be asphyxiated.

I watched television night and day. Ordinarily I like stories of crime, detection, and suspense, but the ones I tuned in were too complicated or too harrowing. I found I couldn't stand to watch anyone being handcuffed or bound or gagged or choked. Also I couldn't follow the plots.

Then one day I happened on a series I had never watched before. It was about two youths who rescue a girl from modern pirates in the Caribbean. It was great. I don't remember what the series was called, but it was based on the old "Hardy Boys" books for juveniles.

I had regressed that far.

I tried to watch the Dodgers, but sometimes they weren't on TV, and when they were, they were usually playing so badly I almost wished they weren't being televised.

I read, but I couldn't stay with anything but detective novels filled with sex and violence—and they had to be old ones that I had already read so that I didn't have to work too hard at the plots and didn't get too anxious over the suspense.

I put the Sunday crossword puzzle on the dining table and pecked away at it at breakfast and lunch; but I found that whenever I didn't immediately think of the required word I couldn't stand the frustration, the sense of being trapped in a maze.

Finally, one morning in the last week of school, I got a letterhead and a pen and laboriously wrote a note to the teachers and children of Mt. Washington School, thanking them; it was short and not very eloquent, but I did it.

My wife drove it up to the school and gave it to the principal, who said it was just in time. There was to be an assembly in five minutes, and she would read it.

So the children of Mt. Washington School were not only the first to welcome me home; they were also the first to get me back into circulation.

CHAPTER 3

A Second Chance

Prospects of Being
a Monday-Morning Quarterback

Sunday, January 18, 1987

WHO HAS NEVER SAID or thought "If I had my life to live over again?"

The idea of having one's life to live over again is among the most common of fantasies.

What paragons we would be if only we had a second chance.

Frank Liberman, the veteran publicist, has sent me a set of resolutions attributed to Nadine Stair, 85, of Louisville, Ky. It is a list of changes she would make in her life if she had it to live over again.

"I'd dare to make more mistakes next time. I'd relax. I would limber up. I would be sillier than I have been this trip. I would take fewer things seriously. I would take more chances. I would perhaps have more actual troubles, but I'd have fewer imaginary ones...."

And so on. Obviously, if Nadine Stair could start over again, she'd kick up her heels some, quit worrying, be daring, have more fun. Damn the consequences!

I suppose most of us would use a second chance the same way.

The idea of going back to some particular time and rearranging the future has great appeal. It was the theme of two recent movies, "Back to the Future" and "Peggy Sue Got Married." In the first, the hero tries to turn his nerd of a father into a real man; in the second, the heroine has a sexual adventure with the class poet and tries to head off the nerd she married.

I have probably mooned about starting over as much as anyone else. One thing I know I would do: I'd save my money and get rich.

All of us can look back to certain crossroads that changed our lives. For one thing, I got married, too. My life has never been the same.

Early in 1944, when I was employed at the United Press bureau in Sacramento, I got tired of being the only civilian in Buddy Baer's bar. One day I telephoned my draft board and insisted on being drafted.

A year later I found myself crouching in a shell hole on Iwo Jima, with Japanese mortar shells bursting all about, wondering how I could have made such a stupid mistake.

In the fall of 1942, I had left a job with the Honolulu Advertiser, worked briefly for the Honolulu Star-Bulletin, then come back to the States. If I had stayed at the Advertiser, I might have become editor of that paper and lived a life of distinction in the Islands, having my gin and tonic every evening in my home on Diamond Head and entertaining the cream of visitors from around the world.

Everywhere, people would say: "You're going to the Islands? Look up Jack Smith. Marvelous old chap."

Our parlor, like George Washington's, would never be empty.

Nadine Stair said: "I've been one of those persons who never goes anywhere without a thermometer, a hot water bottle, a raincoat and a parachute. If I had to do it again, I would travel lighter than I have...."

I don't know. Maybe I've traveled too light. I have quit several jobs without knowing where I was going to land. Maybe a parachute would have come in handy.

In 1937, I was going to sea in the Merchant Marine. I was the lowest form of marine life—a scullion—on the SS Monterey. At the end of two voyages to the Antipodes, I telephoned my father from San Francisco and told him I was about to sign on a President liner and go 'round the world. He persuaded me to come back to Bakersfield and go to college.

That was a mistake. I did not do well in college, though I became editor of the college newspaper and got a job on the Bakersfield Californian. But I have always wondered what my life would have been like if I'd gone 'round the world and stayed with the sea. I might have become a character out of Maugham or Conrad.

Of course, if I hadn't gone back to Bakersfield, I wouldn't have met my wife.

On the other hand, I'd probably have a wife in every port. Not better. But different.

What if I'd stayed on the Advertiser? Instead of becoming a distinguished figure, known 'round the world for my cellar, my hospitality and my informed, sophisticated, global conversation, I might have degenerated into a lush, wasting away in dry rot while my children turned into beach bums and my wife went to an early grave in humiliation, disappointment and regret.

Oh, if I had a second chance, I might eliminate a few minor peccadilloes. I might not make all the fatuous remarks I've made at cocktail parties. I would certainly try not to hurt the people I have hurt.

But I am what I am, as Popeye says. And I doubt that I could change very much.

Or would want to.

Semper fidelis.

Down Memory Lane in an
Old Book Cart

Monday, April 15, 1991

I WENT BACK in time with my cousin Annabel recently, back to the late 1920s in Shafter, when we were both small children.

Shafter is a farm center 18 miles northwest of Bakersfield. Annabel grew up there. It is a small town now; it was a smaller town then. It had no fast-food joints, no bars, no movie theater, no high school.

It had a women's club and a library. On Saturday nights the women's club showed a movie. My cousin Donald accompanied the movie on the player piano. He tried to suit the piano roll to the mood. When anyone died, he played "Nearer My God to Thee." That was the height of culture in Shafter in the 1920s.

Annabel's mother, my Aunt Effie, was librarian for 35 years, beginning in 1925. We lived in Bakersfield at the time, a metropolis. In the summer, and sometimes on weekends, my father drove me out to visit Annabel. We were best friends.

I remember walking over the sandy soil (it was mined with treacherous stickers) to the library. It was a substantial-looking V-shaped red brick building with an arched doorway. When my Aunt Effie went home to water her plants, Annabel and I had the run of the place.

We used to duel with the slitted poles on which newspapers are hung. We pushed each other around on the oak book cart. One dreadful morning I crashed it into a desk, causing visible damage. We covered the splintered edge with spit and prayed that Aunt Effie wouldn't notice it. She didn't. Aunt Effie could be a terror when angry.

Annabel and I were drawn back to Shafter by the 25th anniversary celebration of the *new* library, which was built on the site of the old library in 1966. Annabel left Shafter in 1952.

The ceremony was held on the concrete apron in front of the library. It was not a large crowd. We sat on folding chairs. My Aunt Effie's former assistant, Mary Neufeld Epp, recalled that when the new library was finished the old book cart, along with all the stored books, was moved into it.

I looked at Annabel. We had the same thought. Surely the old book cart that we had desecrated could not still exist! After the ceremony we looked for the cart. There it stood, behind the main desk. It was obviously very old and had seen much abuse. Were we part of its ignominious history?

Annabel wanted to go looking for her roots. It was amazing how many of the old landmarks remained. We found the house she lived in, still in use. Her world had been close about her. She was circled by friends. She could walk to visit them. She watched the blacksmith shoe horses; the barber kidded her about her freckles and her "golden hair"; the postmistress let her know when a shipment of baby chicks was coming in; she knew the owner of the drug store; she used to watch the filling station owner pump gas, literally, and choose a Delaware Punch from a barrel full of ice and pop; she watched the Santa Fe go by, throwing off a canvas sack of mail and snatching the outgoing sack from a pole; sometimes, at the depot, they pulled her around on a big baggage wagon with iron wheels; she could walk into the general store where her father worked behind the counter, helping herself to a cracker from the cracker barrel. (Her father was more often paid in groceries than in cash, and her mother had to board the seasonal potato buyers to make ends meet.)

The old Santa Fe depot had been moved a few blocks and turned into a museum. Among the old pieces of railroad equipment on display was a rough-hewn baggage wagon with iron wheels. Annabel was sure it was the one she had ridden on. It must have been as old as the book cart.

The corner where the general store had stood was now the Casino Bar.

Annabel recalled that for a time her parents had not had a telephone. When they had to make a call they used the phone of a neighbor. One day Annabel's mother told her to go telephone her father and tell him to bring home bread and lettuce.

Annabel was excited. She had never used a telephone before. When the operator said the customary "Number, please," she froze. She couldn't remember the store's number. She said, "Bring home bread and lettuce" and hung up, mortified.

She was afraid to tell her mother. But the day was saved. Her father came home with bread and lettuce. The operator had recognized Annabel's voice and had rung up her father to give him the vital message.

No wonder Annabel felt secure.

Those days are gone forever.

Chalking One Up for an A Student

Monday, August 8, 1994

THE REUNION of the Belmont High School classes of Winter and Summer 1934 was an unqualified success.

We had about 100 guests in our house—classmates of mine and their spouses.

We had hired a valet parking service, figuring our hill would be too steep for our visitors, and my wife had rented four sets of tables and chairs to be sure that people would have a place to sit down. As usual at large parties, most people congregated in the living areas of the house, around the punch bowl, so to speak, ignoring the outside tables.

The party consisted mostly of nostalgic conversation, whoops of recognition, hugs and a few tears.

We even sang the old school alma mater:

There's a school of beauty rare
On top of old Crown Hill,
We're never shy, it's Belmont High....

My wife and I were astonished that so many people came, that so many of my classmates were still alive, still active, still enthusiastic—some of them still beautiful. There were a few signs of frailty. One walker, several canes, including mine. But most of the guests were on their feet and bouncy.

I won't mention any names. I would have to leave some out, and nobody should be left out.

As I sat in my chair greeting old friends, inevitably I thought of those old days. They were hard Depression years. I started at Belmont as a sophomore, having done my freshman year at Whittier High School. I lived with my mother and father in the Prince Rupert apartments at the foot of the hill, near the Mayfair Hotel.

I was a good student. I got straight A's in Latin and English, although I wasn't so good in geometry and science. We had a senile geometry teacher who especially disliked me. He always punctuated his rambling dissertations with the word *portion*, whose meaning in his context no one ever understood. He would often stare at me and then throw a piece of chalk at me.

My journalism teacher, as I have said here, knew nothing about journalism, and we made her life miserable. Nevertheless, that's where I got my start, being editor of the Belmont Sentinel.

Our principal, Mr. Benshimol, was a stern but compassionate man. He tried to make gentlemen of us boys. He decreed that we must wear neckties every day. I both obeyed and protested this rule by coming to school in a bright red satin shirt with a bright orange necktie.

In my senior year I was center on the lightweight (Class B) basketball team. I was high point man for the year with a total of 48 points in six games. (Michael Jordan used to make 48 points in one game.)

In the beginning my family was prosperous. My father was in the investment business. He drove a Graham-Paige, which I often borrowed to take girls to the dances. It was an impressive chariot.

Later my father bought me a 1929 Ford roadster. That day I became a man. As the Depression deepened, my father's business went downhill. Finally it collapsed entirely and he skipped, leaving my mother and me destitute. I had to sell the Ford. We moved in with my sister, who lived in Long Beach. She had a lovely contralto voice and had a sustaining program on KFOX, making $25 a week. We lived on it.

The 1933 earthquake wrecked Long Beach Poly High, and I dropped out of school until the next semester, when we moved back to L.A. and I went back to Belmont. My grades were a shambles. I had been an A student in Latin. I flunked. My Latin teacher cried.

I continued to get A's in English, and my English teacher, a Miss Keyes, told me: "Boy, you can write." I think those words of encouragement steered me into my career.

In time my father came back to rejoin society and re-established himself in real estate in Bakersfield. He wanted to put me through college. My career at Bakersfield College was spotty. I did become editor of the college newspaper, the Renegade Rip, which further defined my future. I dropped out of college to work as a sportswriter on the Bakersfield Californian and am still trying to write.

Looking through my Belmont yearbook during the party, I couldn't help noticing that all the girls, as well as the teachers, wore dresses considerably below the knee—in fact, just above the ankles. Those skirts were uniformly unattractive. At the same time, other pictures showed the same girls wearing shorts on the basketball court, their long legs flashing quite unshielded. I didn't understand it then, and I don't understand it now.

At about 2 o'clock on Sunday, the day after the party, a classmate of mine appeared at our doorway with his wife.

"Do you know where Jack Smith lives?" his wife asked.

After 60 years, they were 24 hours late.

Circus Excitement Is Still Intents

Monday, November 5, 1990

W E T O O K our three younger grandchildren the other day to the Cirque du Soleil at the Santa Monica pier.

It is not the circus that played in every American city and hamlet for a century. There were no wild animals, no horses. There was no fat lady, no tattooed man, no Tom Thumb.

But the acrobats and the trapeze artists were absolutely amazing, and the clown, between the acts, reminded us that pantomime can be hilarious.

It is miraculous that the circus is alive at all today, with the competition of TV and big-time sports. The crowd sat on hard bleacher seats under a striped tent, but no one left early, and after the last act they roared for minutes, bringing the ensemble back for three curtain calls.

Perhaps I feel especially drawn to the circus because it might have been my calling. When I was 10 years old someone gave me a kids' novel named "Andy the Acrobat" for my birthday. It was the first full-length book I had ever read. It was about a boy my age who left home and joined a traveling circus.

Naturally, the book had a great influence on me. I thought of running away from home and joining a circus myself. I was definitely drawn toward the life. But I was also fascinated that anyone could write so many words as the author of that book. Instead of joining a circus, I decided to be a writer. Perhaps my life has not been as exciting as it might have been, but if I had followed the circus I would never have lived in the same house for 40 years, as I have.

No event was greater in small-town America than the coming of the circus. It usually came by train, unloading all its animals and props on a siding at night. In the morning, it paraded through town—elephants, horses, acrobats, tigers—the whole glorious troupe. Meanwhile, roustabouts were pitching the big top on some vacant corner, and for two days the town was in thrall.

There were few boys who didn't try to climb under the tent for a free show. Usually they were caught by the circus bulls. The punishment was slight. Sometimes a kid was allowed to work his way in by watering the elephants.

When I was a youth I worked for part of a summer as a bellhop in a hotel in Willows, in the Sacramento Valley. During my time there a circus came to town, and its people stayed in the hotel. I was thrilled to be in their service. I took ice to the rooms of those fabulous people—bandsmen, trapeze girls, clowns, acrobats, the ringmaster. They were all down-to-earth but exceedingly polite. There was no bad conduct. In fact, I do not remember ever hearing of circus people committing crimes or disturbing the peace while visiting small towns.

Movies have been made about the circus life. Inevitably, there must be alliances and jealousies among such hard-working and dedicated people—people who have chosen to abandon home and stability for the road. This may be what makes them so fascinating to the rest of us.

One is transfixed as the trapeze girl leaves her swinging high ring, makes two somersaults and is caught at the wrists by the man who is swinging toward her on his ring. The timing is exquisite. The body control is breathtaking. One wonders whether the two are lovers, or whether she hates him, and whether it's mutual.

During one such exercise their hands missed, and she fell into the safety net. Immediately she climbed to her high perch again and swung out once more to a mid-air rendezvous. This time he caught her and the crowd sighed. Was the miss deliberate? To heighten the crowd's anxiety? I doubted it. The trick looked impossible to begin with. I couldn't see how they did it.

One reason for the fascination of the circus, I imagine, is the wonder we feel that fellow human beings have developed such incredible control of their bodies. We wonder whether we could ever have done such things, if we had started down a different path.

We marvel at the skill of a third baseman scooping up a hard grounder and throwing out a batter at first base. But it's child's play compared with the skill of the girl on the high trapeze. (I hope I will be excused for calling her a girl. *Trapeze woman* just doesn't sound right.)

There was also the young woman who lay on her back and twirled four parasols simultaneously, two with her feet and two with her hands. And the four exceedingly lissome young women who tied themselves in knots and formed a pyramid of living pretzels.

I doubt that I ever could have trained my body to work on the high trapeze, but, what the heck, I might have made it as a clown.

At least I could have watered the elephants.

Trip to Charlie's a Real Blowout

Sunday, August 10, 1986

THIS IS THE SUMMER, we are told, that Americans are discovering America in greater numbers than ever.

Scared away from foreign travel by terrorism, we are exploring our own country by the tens of millions.

Our efficient cars, our endless freeways and our ubiquitous motels have made it possible for any family to cover from 200 to 400 miles of geography a day, depending on the pace.

Add our handy credit cards, which give us the illusion that it's free.

Never in history have a people enjoyed such travel within their national boundaries.

My wife and I recently traveled into Northern California and back, never worried about the performance of our car, about where we would stay, about how we would pay.

We just drove on, picking destinations from our road map, and in late afternoon we would find some inn with a "Vacancy" sign, show our credit card and put up for the night. Sometimes we had a pool and a hot tub. Often free ice. And always TV, which we never watched. Not watching TV, we found, was a part of being on vacation.

It was so easy I couldn't help remembering the trip my family made from Whittier to Joplin, Mo., back in 1929.

We set out in early summer in our Oakland sedan—my mother, my grandmother, my older brother Harry, my cousin Betty Mae and I.

My brother was a student at Whittier College. Being the only driver, he drove every mile of the way—a heroic performance.

As I remember, my grandmother was 75 years old. Her youngest son, Charlie, who had been maimed and blinded at 21 in a mining accident, was working a 40-acre farm in the Ozarks and she wanted to see him before she died.

We took U.S. Highway 66. It was an arduous trip. The Oakland was a good car for its day, but it had no air conditioning. The highway was only two or three lanes and in many places only gravel.

We never knew where we were going to spend the night. Motels were a brand-new thing in those days. They were mostly courts of small cottages, mostly without inside plumbing. Sometimes, in small towns, we stayed in private houses whose owners were trying to eke out a living by renting out rooms and offering "home cooking."

Somewhere in Arizona we pulled off the road into a real ghost town. We walked through a swinging door into what had been the saloon. The long bar and the mirrored back bar were still in place. It looked like the set of a hundred Westerns we had seen. There was not another human being in town.

Today, if that place still exists, there will be three motels on either side of it, the saloon will be a restaurant, and every other old building in the community will have been "restored" into a restaurant or a souvenir shop. Buses will pull up, disgorging tourists; there will be a fake mine, a chamber of commerce, a newspaper and at least half a dozen art galleries.

We drove through Arizona, New Mexico, the Texas

panhandle and Oklahoma—all of them great wastes of land. I think it was when we crossed into Missouri that we encountered mud so deep that we made only 10 miles that day.

My grandmother weighed less than 100 pounds, but she was tough. As a young wife she had crossed from Kentucky to Colorado in a covered wagon and had encountered hostile Indians. She never complained.

My uncle Charlie was scratching out a living on his 40 acres with his wife, Elsie, and two small sons. Because of Charlie's blindness, Elsie and the older son did most of the work, plowing the earth with Molly, their only horse, and harvesting their paltry crop with the help of neighbors.

Uncle Charlie was absolutely thrilled by the Oakland. He had never ridden in a car before. We drove him into town one day. He sat in the front seat by my brother; Elsie sat in back. My brother drove faster and faster.

"How fast we a-goin' now?" my uncle shouted.

"Forty!" my brother said.

"You hear that, Elsie?" my uncle shouted back. "We're a-goin' 40!"

Returning to California was harder than going east. It was so hot crossing the desert that we hung wet towels in the windows to cool the air.

The last day, we had six flat tires. Every time a tire blew, my brother and I would have to get out, jack up the car, remove the wheel, remove the tube, patch the tube, put it back in the tire, pump it up, put the wheel back on the car and set out once again, waiting for the next blowout.

If I'm not mistaken, my grandmother died soon after we got home. But she had seen Uncle Charlie. Mission accomplished.

And we did it without a credit card.

American Cities That Bubble With Romance

Sunday, March 26, 1989

KORBEL, the California champagne company, recently commissioned a study to determine the 10 most romantic cities in America.

Not surprisingly, San Francisco was first. The others, in order, were Honolulu, Los Angeles, West Palm Beach, New York, Miami, Rochester, N.Y., San Diego, Boston and Grand Rapids, Mich.

I'm not sure I accept the validity of Korbel's list, because it was based on such inconclusive factors as the number of marriages per capita; per capita sales of flowers, diamonds and champagne; the number of good restaurants and theaters; the miles of shoreline, and the number of sunny days.

I suggest that the amount of champagne sold in any city would be more an indication of its affluence than of its romantic ambiance.

It was champagne sales, however, along with miles of shoreline and number of sunny days, that put San Francisco, Los Angeles and San Diego in the Top 10.

I question also the weight given to the number of marriages. I suspect that people often marry as much out of boredom, frustration and a desire to escape their situations as for any romantic compulsions.

I have never been in West Palm Beach, Rochester or Grand Rapids, but I have had some experience in the other Top 10 cities, and I would not argue with their inclusion on the list.

In the early 1940s we lived for two years in Honolulu, and

its balmy weather, its flowers, music, beautiful scenery and people were indeed romantic.

San Francisco is high on my list. It was from San Francisco that so many of us sailed to war in the Pacific, leaving our wives or girlfriends behind. Our last recollections of home were the cable cars, the view from the Top of the Mark, the cozy little bars and restaurants, the style and energy of the natives. It seemed to have all that was best about America.

I left my wife early one morning and caught a cab for my ship. She was standing on a curb on Powell Street in front of our hotel. She was pregnant. We didn't know if we would ever see each other again.

If romance is aching and poignant, and sad, that moment was romantic.

I came back on an aircraft carrier to San Diego.

The local high school band was playing. Hundreds of citizens had turned out to cheer us.

On my discharge, I took a job as a reporter on the San Diego Journal, and my wife and I set up housekeeping, with our first son, in a GI shack. I doubt that we ever drank champagne then, but I drank a lot of beer.

Still, in my book, the most romantic city in America is the city in which I met and courted my wife.

She had grown up there, the daughter of French immigrants. Her childhood had been frugal. She was still a high school student when I met her on a blind date that was arranged by a mutual friend.

For me, it was love at first sight.

Our courtship was incredibly romantic. I was a dashing figure—a sports reporter on the local daily.

Every Wednesday night we went to the wrestling matches at Steve Strelich's stadium. The wrestlers came up from Los

Angeles by bus. Their matches were staged and phony. But we were young, and every experience was romantic. On Friday nights we went to the same stadium for the fights.

I can't say that my wife ever actually *warmed* to the Wednesday wrestling matches or the Friday fights, but as long as she was at my side, I supposed, she was happy.

My wife had never eaten out when we met. I sometimes took her to Tiny's coffee shop, where I, being sophisticated, had two martinis while she had a glass of Coca-Cola.

We often went to the Fox Theater, and I remember that it was there that we saw "Gunga Din," as romantic a movie as was ever made.

Sometimes, after she finished work at the Owl Drug Store, we would drive up into Kern County Park to park in the dark under the trees by the river and engage in what was then called heavy petting.

Yes, San Francisco, San Diego and Los Angeles indeed have their romantic character; but to me, the most romantic city in America will always be Bakersfield.

Recalling the 4th of July
In the Good Old Days

Tuesday, July 4, 1989

I DON'T LIKE to say that things aren't what they used to be, but I doubt that there will ever be another Fourth of July like the ones we had when I was a small boy.

They were raucous, exhausting and super-patriotic. In the 1920s, World War I was fresh in everyone's mind. It had been, after all, the war to end war, and most of us believed it.

In the eyes of a small boy, World War I was the noblest event in history; it was the Holy Grail. American doughboys had sailed the Atlantic to save the world ("Goodbye Broadway, Hello France!" "Lafayette, we are here!").

Somehow that war stayed in our minds longer than World War II did later on. After World War II we were so horrified by the revelations of the Holocaust, and so frightened by the specter of the nuclear Armageddon, that any romantic feelings about the war itself were subdued.

But we all felt good about World War I. The American Legion was an organization of veterans with enormous political power. We looked with forbearance on their juvenile high jinks in gratitude for their heroism.

Boys my age collected souvenirs of that war. I had a genuine doughboy helmet and a wooden model of a Springfield rifle. For hours on end I played at war in our back yard, going "over the top" and invariably dying in the end. I was rather a theatrical lad, and very good at dying. My abiding fear was that there would be no war when I was old enough to fight. I needn't have worried.

I remember an incident with my father. Riding beside him one day in his Wills Sainte Claire, I asked him if he thought there would be a war for me when I grew up. I have never forgotten the anger that crossed his face. It is one of my strongest impressions of him. He said, "Damn it! Nobody wants another war!" I was cowed, and from that point on I believe I looked less favorably on soldiering as a career.

In 1925, we had no notion that the Treaty of Versailles had irreparably divided Europe, and that the seeds of the next war were already planted. Even when we declined to join the League of Nations we thought, "Good. Best keep out of it."

We were in our era of wonderful nonsense. The nation was

prosperous. The stock market was climbing. President Coolidge said, "The business of America is business." On Broadway the Marx Brothers were cavorting in "The Cocoanuts." Everybody was singing "Yes, Sir, That's My Baby!" Lou Gehrig joined the Yankees. In Germany, "Mein Kampf" was published.

I have vivid memories of the Fourth of July in Bakersfield. As usual in July, it was unmercifully hot. Chester Avenue was like melted wax. Painted crosswalks wavered and the soldiers' boots left depressions in the pavement.

But every small town in America could still turn out an impressive company of doughboys, and they still marched with vigor, like conquering heroes. They were still young and lithe, and their uniforms still fit. We stood on the hot sidewalks and cheered them as they marched past.

The bands were typical small town bands, heavy on the oompahs and full of spirit as they pumped away at "The Star-Spangled Banner," "It's a Long Way to Tipperary," "The Stars and Stripes Forever" and "Over There."

Ahead of the doughboys came first the thinning troop of Civil War veterans. If they had been 20 when that war ended they would have been 80 then. They teetered precariously along the soft street, bumping into one another, but still wearing their old uniforms, blue and gray, with pride.

Then came the Spanish-American War veterans; middle-aged, but still vigorous, and their contingent was large. At last count, only one was left in the nation.

When one remembers the Yankees parading down Broadway or down the Champs Elysees after the reconquest of Paris, it is hard to realize that one day we will all be gone.

After the parade, we all retired to the city parks to picnic on tubs of fried chicken and barrels of ice cream. Despite Prohibition, our fathers drank home brew and became noisily patriotic.

Things didn't turn out the way we thought they would; but we still have something to celebrate. We are still free.

Iwo Jima as Witnessed by a Human Marine

Thursday, August 30, 1990

B Y   T H E   T I M E you read this, it will probably be out of date. I want to say something about the crisis in the Middle East; but of course it changes every hour, and events quickly overtake predictions.

I believe I have read every word printed in The Times about it, including the pontifications of Henry Kissinger. I envy our reporters who are on the scene in Jordan, Kuwait and Saudi Arabia.

I notice, though, that reporters often quote Pentagon or Administration sources who ask to remain anonymous. Also, our commitment to the Middle East is most often expressed in terms of technology.

The other day, for example, a Page 1 story reviewed our military situation in Saudi Arabia. It said that our forces there "include the 7th Marine Expeditionary Brigade, equipped with tanks, heavy artillery and Cobra attack helicopters, and attack-oriented naval forces aboard aircraft carriers armed with A-6 attack bombers, F-18s and EA-6 attack bombers, and EA-6B radar jamming planes...."

Well, that sounds great. If it comes down to a military confrontation, our technology should prevail.

But so far I haven't read much about the human factor. War is fought, in the end, by people. My only experience with it was the battle of Iwo Jima, but I still remember it in human terms. We were told that the reason for attacking Iwo was to secure it as an emergency landing field for B-29 bombers returning from their devastating raids on Tokyo. And I remember seeing the first B-29 land. For that we paid 7,000 dead marines.

My battalion approached Iwo on an LST (landing ship-tank). The weather was bad. Being overcrowded, many of us had to sleep topside, in our bags. When the gale came, we were doused. But one of us, a man named Blake, had ingenuity and foresight. He had rigged up a tent, using blankets and sticks, and came out dry the next day. "I build my house of bricks," he said, smiling slyly.

Blake wanted to be a chemical engineer. I think he would have been a good one. He was blown away on D-day.

I was scheduled to land in the third wave, at 0910. We landed at 0910, exactly. One of the men in my boat looked up at an airplane and his helmet fell off into the ocean. A Navy patrol boat came alongside and a swabbie (marine talk for sailor) gave his helmet to the embarrassed marine. (By the way, he survived.)

I scrambled into a fox hole. I was soon joined by a man named Zimmy. He was a Czech, a banker from Chicago. His specialty was the ability to speak Japanese. It didn't seem to be of much use at the moment. I said, "Funny place for a bad Czech to turn up." He didn't laugh. We dug a common foxhole and survived the night, surrounded by mortar shells.

In the morning I wandered out into an unsecured zone. Suddenly I realized that I was being shot at. I heard the crack of bullets passing. "Crazy," I thought. "Why would anybody want to kill me?"

Later I found our battalion headquarters. The colonel and the captain were eating some canned sausage. "Why don't you go have some," the colonel suggested, "with the enlisted men?"

I excused myself. A few minutes later the colonel stood up to study the Japanese positions through his field glasses. A mortar shell landed nearby. The colonel was killed.

I had a specialty. I was a combat correspondent. I carried a rifle and was supposed to shoot the enemy. But my primary duty was to write stories about individual marines for their home town newspapers. There were two of us in every regiment. The other man in my regiment was Barberio. Everybody loved him. He was full of life and he loved to eat.

We were supposed to carry our Corona portable typewriters with us in the assault. I remember the morning we embarked. Barberio was loaded with everything required, and someone had to give him a push to get him going.

I balked. I went to the colonel and said, "Sir, I am supposed to carry my typewriter ashore with me." He said, "You will not."

The colonel suggested that I send my typewriter in his Jeep, which was scheduled to go in the eighth wave. The boat was sunk. I never saw my typewriter again.

Barberio was killed on D-day. A marine salvaged his typewriter, and offered it to me. I felt guilty. Barberio had gone by the book. I had not. I used my knife to open the case. There was no typewriter in it. It was full of canned goods.

That's what war is like. Only a thousand times worse.

The Irreverent Front-Page Era

March 7, 1990; December 3 and 4, 1991

IN 1931 I saw Pat O'Brien as Hildy Johnson in the first movie version of "The Front Page," and my fate was sealed. I wanted to be the kind of quick-thinking, fast-talking, hard-drinking newspaper reporter that O'Brien was in that classic, and that's what I became.

"Reporters: Memoirs of a Young Newspaperman" by Will Fowler is the book every newspaper reporter of the late 1940s and early 1950s meant to write but didn't. Now Fowler has.

It's as boisterous, irreverent, virile, sentimental and vainglorious as all of us were who worked on newspapers in that last gasp of the Front Page era. Will and I worked together for three years on the Herald-Express, a paper that gloried in sex, crime and wrongdoing, and I can verify that most of his stories are true.

At the Examiner, Will worked for the sadistic Jim Richardson, the worst kind of drunk—a reformed one. Richardson was humorless and tyrannical, but a good city editor.

There were no such things as "investigative reporters" in those days. Every reporter was an investigative reporter. Will once interviewed a young woman who was suicidal because her husband was two years overseas in the war and, though virtuous, she had turned up pregnant. Will kept probing and finally found out that the wife had had a tooth filled months before and the dentist had used gas to put her under. Police records showed that the dentist had previously been accused of rape but was acquitted. Under interrogation he admitted raping the soldier's anesthetized wife in the dental chair. He went to prison.

Will was the first reporter on the scene when Elizabeth Short's dismembered body was found in a grassy lot west of the Coliseum. He and a photographer had been returning from another story when they heard a police broadcast directing cops to the scene. Will and his photog got there first and had to explain themselves when the cops showed up.

As they neared the body, Will called to his photographer, "Jesus, Felix! This woman's cut in half!"

"It is difficult to describe two parts of a body as being one," he writes. "However, both halves were facing upward. Her arms were extended above her head. Her translucent blue eyes were only half-opened so I closed her eyelids."

There are a few errors of fact in "Reporters," which is not unexpected in a book so full of detail and so dependent on memory. Clara Phillips (the Tiger Woman) did not hammer her faithless lover to death; she hammered her faithless husband's lover to death.

Only one other error is important. Will credits Bevo Means, the Herald Sheriff's beat reporter, as the first in getting Elizabeth Short's nickname, the Black Dahlia, into print. No, I was.

Elizabeth used to live in Long Beach and hung out at a drugstore soda fountain with her friends. The pharmacist told police that, because of her bouffant black hairdo and black clothes, they called her the Black Dahlia. Bevo probably called this electrifying piece of news to his desk about the same time our police reporter called it into mine. Recognizing the Black Dahlia for the dramatic sobriquet it was, I immediately wrote a new lead for the story and we went to press. The Daily News being a round-the-clock paper, we got it on the street first.

Since that is probably the only contribution I have made to history, I want the record straight.

Will was not above the tricks we used to get pictures. When the wealthy La Canada socialites Walter and Beulah Anne

Overell were blown up in their yacht at Newport Beach, Will's desk was screaming for a picture of Overell. Will and his photographer found him in the morgue, propped him up and took his picture. The paper's artist opened his eyes and painted in a shirt, necktie and coat. No other paper had it.

Fowler inevitably includes a chapter on marvelous Agness Underwood, city editor of the Herald-Express and the nation's first woman city editor.

Agness had started out as a phone operator on the old Daily Record, but watched her chances and soon had a job as a reporter. Aggie's energy, ingenuity and intuition were legendary. After she had scooped the Herald-Express on five straight stories they surrendered by giving her a job and a raise of $2.50 a week.

Aggie demanded nothing more from her reporters than absolute loyalty and a reverent devotion to the job. She did not insist on absolute sobriety. She did not often drink as city editor, but when she had a rare hangover she would have a case of beer sent up to her desk, and when we reporters showed up at 6 o'clock she would demand that we start the day with a bottle of beer.

When the Her-Ex was merged with the Examiner, Aggie was made assistant managing editor. The managing editor, Don Goodenow, put her in a hot, tiny office in the poorly air-conditioned building and gave her nothing to do. One summer morning, when the slaves on the copy desk were sweltering, Aggie sent out for a case of beer. Soon Goodenow called her to his office.

"Are they drinking beer out there?" he asked her.

"Yes, they are," she answered.

"Well, go tell them to stop it."

"You go tell them yourself, you son-of-a-bitch," said Aggie. "I bought it for them."

Fowler recalls that I once told him how I got my job at the Her-Ex, explaining that "I have never told the story before because it isn't exactly an example for the young."

Fowler wrote: "He (Smith) said he had left the Daily News for another paper which soon folded.

" 'So in keeping with tradition,' he said, 'I went to the press club to celebrate.' "

Assistant city editor Art McCarroll had been phoning around for Jack to come to work at the Her-Ex.

" 'But I wasn't ready to go back to work,' said Smith. 'My paper had just folded and I was supposed to celebrate.'

" 'Aggie wants to talk to you,' " said McCarroll after locating Smith.

" 'Tell her I'm drunk,' " said Smith.

"Jack heard Art speaking away from the phone. 'Aggie, Smith says he's drunk.' A second later, McCarroll was back to Smith. 'Aggie wants to know when you'll be able to start work.'

" 'Monday,' Smith said. And he showed up sober on Monday."

Rewriteman Dick O'Connor once told Fowler, "Never have a hangover on your own time."

Evidently taking this to heart, Will showed up one morning with a dreadful hangover and had to take an obituary over the phone from an old friend of the deceased. He kept questioning the caller, asking him who he was and what he did and so on, and finally wrote an obituary about the caller, not about the dead man.

When it was published the subject was furious. He threatened to sue. Aggie sent Will out to see him with a bottle of Scotch. Will called Aggie to tell her that the man had changed his tune. He was delighted with the obit. He wanted it brought up-to-date and published when he died.

"It's a promise," Aggie said.

He also wanted to frame it, Will said.

"Buy the frame," said Aggie.

Here's to the Gallant Press: They'll Drink to That!

Thursday, April 5, 1990

H E R B K R A U C H of Gilman Hot Springs confirms, with others, that during Prohibition distilled spirits could be obtained by prescription, "for medicinal purposes only," but throughout that noble experiment "most newspapermen drank bootleg gin."

Nobody would know more about the habits of newspapermen in the Prohibition era than Krauch. Herb is 93. He spent 50 years on the Herald-Express, starting in 1912 as an office boy at $4 a week and rising to editor.

I worked as a reporter under Krauch in the early 1950s and know something about the drinking habits of reporters myself.

Herb says reporters drank bootleg gin because it was easier to get than prescription booze and a lot cheaper. Since reporters probably made about $25 a week in those days, cheap was important.

"In 1930," he recalls, "we had a house of ill fame across from the Herald on Trenton Street, where one city editor occasionally spent his lunch time, and a bootleg bar at the corner of Trenton and Pico Boulevard.

"If you wanted a drink at the office you could go into the photographic department and Frank Bentley, head photographer, would sell you a shot of gin for 10 cents. In 1928 the city editor was drinking two fifths a day and eventually, in delirium tremens, was carried out of the office on a stretcher. Those were the days."

One wonders whether the quality of the paper was affected by the city editor's going into delirium tremens. We all worked in a sort of constant delirium.

When I worked at the Herald in the early 1950s our city editor was Agness Underwood, a tough, sentimental, competent newspaperwoman who had been a holy terror on the street as a reporter. As city editor Agness rarely drank, but sometimes she would pass out beer to her boys, as a reward for honest labor, from a case that had been delivered from the Continental Bar at Pico and Georgia Street by George Banker, the one-eyed bartender.

The Continental was the longest bar in town. George was gruff and burly, with an intimidating eyeless socket. But he was sweet; he ran the bar like a priest ministering to his flock. It was always clogged with muggers, hookers, bag ladies, used car salesmen from nearby Figueroa Street, and, of course, reporters and photographers. George also kept the permanent stew, food being required by law. No one ever knew what went into it.

We were a disreputable lot, but we kept the people informed, at least about the lower reaches of society. Stanley Walker had defined news as "wine, women and wampum," and we covered it. I have always wanted to print a poem about that breed. I do not know its author, but it was copyrighted in 1928 by the McNaught Syndicate Inc. With apologies to its author:

Here's to the gallant reporters,
Those boys with the pencils and pads,
Those calm, imperturbable, cool,
undisturbable,
Nervy, inquisitive lads.
Each time that we pick up a paper

Their marvelous deeds we should bless;
Those bold, reprehensible, brave,
indispensable
Sensible lads of the press.

Those lines are heavily sentimental and ironic, but they were probably written by one of those bold, reprehensible, brave, indispensable, sensible lads of the press himself.

Of course, there were lassies as well as lads, but not many. The women were often called sob sisters and were usually given tear jerkers to write—stories about young mothers who were in jail for sticking their boyfriends with an ice pick. But they were good reporters—tough, aggressive, resourceful, subtle and fearless.

Agness Underwood, as a reporter, once dropped a white carnation on the body of a waitress who had been stabbed to death in a bar, just to give the story a name—"The White Carnation Murder." Then she told her photographer to take a picture of her creation. A policeman interfered. Agness slapped him with her purse. As a city editor, Agness expected her reporters to be no less aggressive.

The press has now become the media, and its practitioners wear stylish clothes and drink fastidiously. City editors are rarely carried out in delirium tremens. Reporters are responsible family men and women and have degrees.

Or so I hear.

CHAPTER 4

The Family Extended

A Joyeux Introduction to Middle Age

Reprinted from Spend All Your Kisses Mr. Smith, 1978

N O B O D Y K N O W S when middle age begins; not even the doctors and psychologists. It is said to be a state of mind as much as a physical condition, and its victim may be quite well into it before he realizes he is into it at all.

I know exactly the day on which I found out that I had already made this momentous passage, and in fact was well into it: Friday, May 23, 1969, rather late in the afternoon.

My discovery was heralded by the sound of our younger son Doug's motorcycle varooming up the hill. My wife and I heard him stop in front of the house and started out to greet him. He was living at that time in Westwood, where he shared a pad with two other UCLA students, and we were delighted by his occasional visits home.

We heard his familiar voice—young, playful, exuberant— and a second voice, the voice of a young, playful and exuberant girl, but a stranger. It was the first time he had brought a female home on his motorcycle. Usually it was books.

We hurried outside. What we saw unnerved us for a moment. They both wore glossy plastic helmets, his red, hers blue, with plastic visors distorting their faces. They looked like humanoid beetles. He kicked out the parking stand and settled the motorcycle and helped her off. She pulled off her helmet and shook out her hair. It was shoulder-length; a light reddish brown.

She rolled her eyes and made a little theatrical gesture of dismay. "I have ruin my permanent," she sighed.

She wore a shapeless blue windbreaker and blue jeans and

chic brown boots; but despite this camouflage I made two hasty observations: whoever she was, she was full-grown; and she spoke with a French accent. I had a feeling that events of which I had not even been aware had already gone past some point of no return.

We asked them to dinner and they stayed. The young woman's name was Jacqueline Joyeux, the Joyeux being French for "joyous." My sense of inevitability was deepened. Our son was half-French, his mother being the daughter of French immigrants, and it was not surprising that he would be attracted to a girl named Joyeux, perhaps fatally.

Her home was in Tours, and she had come to America, on her own, on a visitor's visa. To prolong her stay she had found work as a maid in a Beverly Hills home, which was of course illegal, and was rooming with a clutch of French girls similarly employed in domestic service. Our son, evidently, had serendipitously come upon this nest of nubile Gallic pigeons and soon cut Mademoiselle Joyeux from the flock. Where it would end one could only guess, and I already had.

They decided to stay the night. Mademoiselle Joyeux was given the privacy of our spare bedroom and our son slept on the couch in my den, an arrangement that was not contested.

"Well," I told Denny when we were alone, "it looks like she might be the one."

"Yes," she said, as if she had always known it.

We were all up early. They put on their helmets, lowered their visors, waved goodbye and trundled off down the hill. Denny and I were left standing in the empty street. The thrum of the motorcycle died out, and suddenly it was very quiet. I felt middle-aged, and slightly square.

Fencing Fancier Catches
Mistair Smees Off Garde

Reprinted from Spend All Your Kisses Mr. Smith, *1978*

W E S A W Mademoiselle Joyeux rather often that summer and fall, mostly on weekends when Doug brought her by on his motorcycle. We were pleased to have her about. Our older son, Curt, was off with the Air Force in Southeast Asia, and we missed him. She helped to fill the house.

Denny had a woman to talk to, in French, and I was entertained by Mademoiselle Joyeux's buoyancy, her vivacity, and her Gallic impertinence. She happily regarded me as the embodiment of everything the French deplored in the American character. I was an easy target. When we fenced, which was often enough that I rather felt myself always en garde, she usually won the point. Her tactics were to pink me with a saucy thrust, unprovoked, as I saw it; and then when I parried, to withdraw behind our language barrier, looking quite innocent, as if *she* were the injured party. Was it *her* fault if I didn't understand English? Meanwhile, she kept me at my distance by calling me Mr. Smith, which came out something like *Mistair Smees.*

I got the impression in those weeks that she was not trying to understand me so much as trying to design me, to make me fit some stereotype for the middle-aged American male, especially one she might be appraising as a possible father-in-law.

She finally placed me in a category, but I wasn't to know what it was until late in October, after Doug had dropped out of college, quit his job and left town on his motorcycle with a vague announcement that he was going to see America before he was drafted. He meant to go all the way to New York.

But we could see that Mademoiselle Joyeux was baffled and perhaps hurt by what must have seemed to her an act of desertion. It was her crisis too. We did not presume to probe or interfere, but we fetched her over to our house one evening for dinner, hoping the familiar setting and the wine and candlelight would make her feel at home and restore her confidence.

We dined outside in the patio. Denny had prepared a small French dinner, and Mademoiselle Joyeux had pitched in as usual to help with the table and make the salad. I started to open a bottle of champagne but thought better of it. Champagne might be too ostentatious, might make it seem that we needed to desperately be cheered up. Instead I chose a Vouvray from the Loire Valley in which Mademoiselle Joyeux had been born and raised.

It was a lovely dinner. The evening was balmy, as October evenings are in Los Angeles. The sunset lingered, and when twilight came I turned on the light in my goldfish tank. The graceful little fish, so quick and vivid, added life and color to the scene, and we finished the wine by candlelight, talking softly.

Whatever anxiety any of us might have felt about our missing Galahad was muted in the conversation. Mademoiselle Joyeux was amiable and piquant. She personified that excellent phrase of her country, *joie de vivre*.

Then suddenly she grew pensive. She leaned toward me across the table, her eyes searching mine. "Mr. Smith," she said, still having trouble with it, pronouncing it *Smees*, "do you think your son will someday be like you?"

It was hardly a question I had anticipated. But I was touched. She was still a child, of course. It was only natural that she would be impressed by maturity. I thought about her question. Would our son someday be like me? Well, what young woman *wouldn't* want her mate to be kind and gentle, with a certain urban polish, a modest affluence, a mixture of dash and prudence, and beyond that, as the French would say, *je ne sais quoi.*

"What do you mean, *mon cher?*" I said gently, hoping the familiar French endearment would make her feel at home.

"You know, Mr. Smith," she said, "*bourgeois.*"

A Father's Day That Pickles His Fancy

Reprinted from Spend All Your Kisses Mr. Smith, 1978

FOR YEARS I have tried to phase out Father's Day. I consider it silly and commercial. If a man had the respect and affection of his wife and children, he would have it every day. If not, there was no use in setting aside one day of the year for perfunctory demonstrations.

But it isn't easy for a father to phase out Father's Day. The more he protests that he doesn't wish to be the object of any extraordinary attentions, the more he is suspected of inviting them. A man who is truly modest and self-effacing is rarely taken seriously.

So I thought of getting at Father's Day through Mother's Day, which fortunately comes first. I simply phased out Mother's Day. It seemed to me that if I gave up Mother's Day, the other members of the family would sooner or later get the idea and give up Father's Day. It's oblique, but I've discovered that in some families the oblique approach is best.

So, I ignored Mother's Day completely, except to give my wife a jar of sweet pickles. Of course that was only a joke. I happen to love sweet pickles in liverwurst sandwiches, but she rarely remembers to keep them in good supply.

I also gave her the annual explanation of my attitude. It was just that I resented being obliged by some nationwide sales pitch to express, through merchandise, an essentially private sentiment engendered by years of proximity and interdependence.

"I know," she said.

I realized I had won her over when she decided to leave me on Father's Day and drive down to our house in Mexico alone. It was a symbolic act of liberation for us both. I could spend the day in solitude, reading and reflecting. Father's Day should be a day for introspection, for adding up one's wins and losses and striking one's balance.

I was carrying out this plan when the phone rang. It was Jacqueline.

"It is you Mr. Smith? You are at home?"

"Yes, of course. I am at home."

"Good. We will see you later."

A few minutes later Curt phoned. "Are you going to be home?" he asked. "I thought I might drop by."

Curt was back in UCLA, determined to finish the education his time in the Air Force had interrupted, and was working on the side as well, so we hadn't been seeing as much of him as we would have liked.

He arrived in an hour with a young woman I hadn't seen before. She had dark hair and dark eyes and a sunniness that made me think of Italy.

"This is Gail Paolucci," Curt said.

They were the Paoluccis of San Fernando Valley now, but they had come from southern Italy a generation or two ago, by way of Buffalo. She looked thoroughly American, this Miss Paolucci, but I had an idea she could put together a proper lasagna. She was taking physical therapy at UCLA, and they had met in chemistry. Evidently some chemistry was already at work. I was reminded of the day Doug had first come up the hill on his motorcycle with Mademoiselle Joyeux.

Curt and Miss Paolucci had brought me a large plastic bag full of water, with a rather fancy goldfish in it.

"For Father's Day," he said.

I had been phasing out my goldfish, much in the way Denny had been phasing out my pickles, by neglecting to replace them as one by one they disappeared. But this was a pretty fish; maybe just what I needed to restore my old enthusiasm.

Soon Doug arrived with Jacqueline, Crisopher, and Jacqueline's sister, Nanette. Nanette was carrying an enormous black puppy with a white spot on his chest.

"Not for me!" I said weakly, trying not to show my dismay.

"He is partly a Labrador retriever," said Jacqueline.

"A retriever?" I said, wanting to say that the last thing in the world I needed was a retriever.

"And part Dalmatian," said Nanette.

"Z'white spot," said Jacqueline, "zat is z'Dalmatian part."

"His name is Stephan," Doug said.

"Stephan?" It was all beginning to seem surreal, like a scene in a bad French movie.

"He's named after Stephan Bandera. You know, the Ukrainian rebel."

My familiarity with Russian history did not encompass Ukrainian rebels.

"He rebelled against the Soviet Union."

Much to my relief it turned out that Stephan Bandera was theirs. They had bought me something else. My daughter-in-law carried the gift into the house in a bulky sack. I viewed it with apprehension, but I knew it couldn't be worse than a dog.

"So you will not give them any more to your wife," she said.

It was three quart jars of pickles. I was touched.

So it turned out to be a rewarding Father's Day after all. I was so relieved not to be getting the Labrador retriever that I drove all six of them down to Venice for a festive Greek dinner at the Cheese and the Olive.

"How do you think the Rams will do this year?" Miss Paolucci asked me as I sipped a glass of retsina.

"Better than last year, I hope," I said.

"I'm afraid they have a quarterback problem," she said. I was astounded. Here was a young woman who not only knew how to cook lasagna, unless I was mistaken, but also understood football well enough to know that the Rams had a quarterback problem. Miss Paolucci, I decided, was a treasure.

I soon grew fond of the goldfish. He would always remind me that he might have been a dog. And I had enough sweet pickles to last me to the next Father's Day, which I hoped to spend alone in quiet introspection.

It's a Good Gail That Blows In on Thanksgiving

Reprinted from Spend All Your Kisses Mr. Smith, 1978

FROM THE BEGINNING, Denny and I sensed that Curt and Gail had serious intentions, and they did not keep us waiting long.

Any doubt about the outcome of their acquaintance was put to rest when she invited us to the home of her parents, far out in the San Fernando Valley, for Thanksgiving dinner. In American culture, a young couple who failed to marry after bringing their parents together at the Thanksgiving table would be seriously compromised.

So it was with that feeling of meeting a new set of relatives-to-be that we drove out to the Paolucci house. Like the Joyeux, Bernie and Mary Ann Paolucci had two daughters, Gail's sister, Bernadette, being also the younger. Thus, when we entered the Paolucci household, the situation was reminiscent of that first evening in Tours.

But this time I was on my good behavior. There would be wine, of course, or Paolucci's name wasn't Paolucci. But there would be no language barrier, so it was not expected that he would ask me to sample every wine of the Italian campagna as a substitute for conversation.

It was evident that Gail was very close to her family, and would remain so, which meant that they would inevitably become a part of our family too. If it was not wine, I wondered what common ground I would have with Bernie Paolucci, or would there, perhaps, be none at all? We were no sooner through their front door than my concern evaporated.

Paolucci and I shook hands, but he seemed to be straining to hear a sound emanating from the door of what appeared to be a man's den, just off the entry hall. I recognized the sound: a crowd roar and the frantic voice-over of the announcer. He had the Ram game on TV.

"What's the score?" I asked.

"Dallas was ahead one touchdown," he said. "But it sounds like something just happened."

We moved into the living room for the perfunctory introductions and exchanges.

"Well, Jack," Bernie said, when the conversation lulled, "we might as well watch the game. They won't need us in the kitchen."

As we headed for Bernie's den, I thought of that great last line in "Casablanca," when Claude Rains and Humphrey Bogart are walking arm in arm into the night, and Bogart says: "Louis, I think this is the beginning of a beautiful friendship."

CHAPTER 5

A Grandfather Rarely Rests

Reader Has His Pick-on-Jack Day

Monday, July 30, 1990

IN WRITING A COLUMN five days a week, year after year, one inevitably reveals more of himself than he may want to.

As impersonal as I try to be, some aspects of my character, my private self, are likely to appear, as in a mirror darkly.

Thus, I would have assumed that I had shown myself as a gentle, thoughtful, helpful and loving husband, father and grandfather, and a good fellow in any society.

But I have not tried to conceal the fact that I dislike gardening, that I am addicted to sex and violence on television, that I attend Philharmonic concerts, the opera and the theater, and that I am an indifferent traveler.

Not a great deal there to like, I admit; on the other hand, I do not think of myself as a wholly unlikable person, and especially not as a cold one.

As I say, however, if one writes about anything at all, one cannot help exposing his innermost nature, if only indirectly.

So perhaps reader Frank Biro of Van Nuys is correct when he complains that "I wonder if at home you are cold and formal with your family and pets?"

Mr. Biro notes that I apparently expect my wife to do the housework, and consider that I have done more than my share if I place a TV dinner in the micro.

I'm afraid Mr. Biro has struck close to the truth on that point. It is true that my wife does most of the housework, what little is left by our one-day-a-week housecleaner. She often consults me on what TV dinner to put in the micro, but the actual act of placing the dinner in the micro is usually left to her.

"I was under the impression," Mr. Biro goes on, "that marriage was cooperative."

Indeed it is. Having been married 51 years, I suggest to Mr. Biro that that fact alone implies that there has been a great deal of cooperation. I may not cook, but my contributions to our mutual well-being have been too numerous to list.

"Then there are your sons' wives. They call you 'Mr. Smith.' Do your grandchildren also stay forbidden to call you 'Grandpa'?"

Only my French daughter-in-law calls me Mr. Smith. My Italian daughter-in-law calls me Jack. My five grandchildren call me "Grandpa," or "Grampa." In my French daughter-in-law's family, a father-in-law was called *monsieur*. She does not care to defer to American tradition in that respect. I am not foolish enough to forbid any of them anything.

It is true that my wife and I do not use terms of endearment. I call her Denny, she calls me Jack. We have never used *honey* or *dear* or *love* or any other such words. If that implies that we are cold, so be it.

I asked my wife if she thought I was cold. She laughed mischievously. The difference between us, I think, is that my glass is half empty, hers is half full.

I asked my French daughter-in-law if she thought I was cold. She said she knew I was not cold, but sometimes I seemed to be off in another world.

That's it exactly. I may sometimes seem aloof, or distracted, not because I am cold, but because I am always thinking about the higher things.

Sometimes I tend to speculate on our origins, on the consolations of religion, on the deterioration of our planet, on the greed that corrupts our society, on the meaning of infinity, on the state of my cardiovascular system, on the curse of racism, on the uncertainty of life, for dogs and human beings alike.

When caught up in these musings I may seem cold, especially if I am in the midst of gaiety; but I assure Mr. Biro and anyone else who cares, that I am none the less high-spirited, good-natured, generous, warm and vulnerable, and all anyone has to do is offer me a glass of wine to bring me around. Sometimes I'm the life of the party.

I do think it might be more dignified, however, if the kids called me grandfather.

A Quiet Game of Hide and Shriek

Wednesday, November 1, 1978

I WAS HOPING for a quiet Sunday so I could do some work. As it turned out, I accomplished almost nothing, but I regained my faith in the perfectibility of man.

My hopes for a perfect day were dashed the moment the day began. I was awakened, in full panic, by a voice so loud I thought it must be God. I was wondering what I could say for myself when the voice died out with a click and I heard a maniacal shriek. It was my granddaughter Alison, who doesn't talk yet, but is clever enough to slip into a person's bedroom in her sleepers at dawn, and turn the television on.

At the instant of awakening I did not remember that our two granddaughters had been left to spend the night with us, so I was not prepared to find them on the scene. I lay in bed awhile, trying to adjust. There was only one advantage that I could think of. The girls had gotten my wife up early, so the coffee was made. I got out of bed and had a cup and hurried through the paper, then shut myself in my study.

I was no sooner at work than the louver doors flew open.

My older granddaughter, Adriana, who is no more mischievous than her cousin but more advanced intellectually, and therefore more dangerous, tiptoed elaborately across the room. She held a finger to her lips, thus making me a conspirator, and hid in the corner behind my electric chair. I could hear her cousin bumping about the house and shrieking. In a minute or so she ran into the room, demonstrating the fact that the human gait is a series of near falls.

I realized they were playing hide and seek. I wanted to betray Adriana and get it over with, but when you are taken into a game of hide and seek, even involuntarily, you are bound by the code. In less than a minute she leaped out from behind the chair with an unnerving scream and gave herself away. She knows, of course, that the game is no fun if the hider isn't found.

The two of them stumbled out of the room in each other's arms, squealing and giggling insanely. "Girls will be girls," I thought, admiring my own magnanimity.

A minute later Alison came in at a fast toddle and hid in the same corner. They did the whole routine as before, with the roles reversed. There was a certain economy in it, I conceded. If you have a good hiding place, why leave it for someplace else?

Finally they went outdoors and I got in a couple of hours at the typewriter, marred only by intermittent entrances and exits for trips to kitchen and bath. But the tension had reached my central nervous system. I put a hand to my forehead. I definitely had a fever. There was nothing to do but go to bed and watch the San Diego-Oakland game.

That evening, after the girls had gone home, we turned on KCET for the taped telecast of Carlo Maria Giulini's debut with the Philharmonic. It was Beethoven's Ninth.

How beautiful it was, so sweet and playful in the early

movements, like a summer morning, but troubled by those quick heart-thumping omens of the storm to come. The eye as well as the ear was enraptured as the camera framed poignant portraits of the faces in the orchestra, of the director's long pliant face, lugubrious and ecstatic, and finally the chorus, men and women, old, young, everyday faces brought together into an almost unbearably joyful climax.

If human beings could work together with such exquisite harmony, toward such a glorious end, and the Chargers could beat Oakland, in the final minute of play, then surely there was a benign God, and hope for the species after all.

How wonderful it was, I thought, to be part of it, and to have two granddaughters.

'Witch Doctor' Keeps Going and Going and....

Wednesday, December 23, 1981

S O M E T I M E S   I   D O U B T that the Creator's plan is infallible, but He certainly was right in arranging for children to be given to young adults, and not to their elders.

We have had our younger pair of grandchildren for the past three days, their parents having gone to New York City for a holiday, but it seems like weeks. I realize that if the Lord, in a moment of grotesque perversity, were to present me and my wife with a little one at this late date, I would have to decline.

Of course my wife would do most of the physical work, in keeping with our traditional division of chores, but I have found out that just the responsibility of attending to the moral and intellectual development of small children involves a lot of wear and tear, on the nerves if not on the flesh.

It isn't that our grandchildren aren't charming, but at their ages—4 and 2—they seem more interested in expressing their faculties for mischief, in sharpening their wills and in forcing their hideous tastes on everyone else, than in radiating joy.

As the older member of this sibling team, my granddaughter is the innovator. It is she who thinks up what to do, and her brother responds in one of two ways—either he is enthusiastically for it, or enthusiastically against it.

Unfortunately, he shares her taste in music. This happens, at the moment, to be fixed on one of the 45 rpm records that I keep in a small album, hidden on a high shelf in my study, as a memento of the 1950s, when our own two sons were children.

These little records are all powerfully nostalgic for me, but it wasn't an era of great popular music—between Glenn Miller and Elvis Presley—and its most eloquent practitioner was the uninhibited Spike Jones, God rest his soul.

But the other night, hoping to entertain myself as well as the grandchildren, I got the album down. My granddaughter thumbed through the records and put a finger, by sheer bad luck, I'm sure, on "Witch Doctor." My blood turned cold.

Of all the novelty numbers of that era just before Elvis seized the souls of our young like Satan himself, "Witch Doctor" was the hit that did the most damage to our nerves. KFWB used to play it every morning, relentlessly, just at the hour when we were all trying to get into the bathroom in preparation for our various enterprises of the day. I can't imagine why I ever actually purchased a record of it, but there it was in the album.

"What's that one?" she asked.

"Witch Doctor," I said, helplessly, unable to deceive her even to save myself from the ordeal I knew was coming.

"Play that."

"I don't like it," I said, realizing instantly that it was the worst thing I could have said.

"I like it," she said. "Play 'Witch Doctor.'"

With great misgivings, I played it. I can't exaggerate how really dreadful it is. It is sung in a sort of sustained yell.

I told the Witch Doctor I was in love with you.

My friend the Witch Doctor he told me what to do.

I can hardly describe the effect this nonsense had on my grandchildren. They screamed in delight, jumped up and down, ran about the room, fell down, did somersaults and inept handsprings, and as soon as it was over they demanded that it be replayed at once.

"One more time," I said, "and that's it."

The result was the same, and it ended with the same demand for an encore. I got up and opened a bottle of Chablis and poured a glass. I was simply not up to another "Witch Doctor" without a tranquilizer. It was a question of which evil was the lesser. I could fortify myself against the nerve damage and play "Witch Doctor" until they tired of it, or I could refuse to play it again and stand by for whatever kind of reprisal they thought up—a terrible dilemma indeed.

I played "Witch Doctor" five more times.

In the morning their parents called from New York to see how they were behaving.

"Fine," I said. "I've been playing 'Witch Doctor.' They love it."

"Oh dear," their mother said. "Can't you play some classics?"

That night I played a little Mozart divertimento; a lovely thing.

"That's yukky," my granddaughter said.

"Yukky," her brother agreed.

You can't teach savages to love Mozart in one weekend. I opened my best Chardonnay and played "Witch Doctor" four more times. Actually, with Chardonnay, it wasn't that bad.

An Interesting Study
of Ploys and Girls

Wednesday, April 2, 1980

I DON'T KNOW whether it's her mother's and father's fault, or mine, but my older granddaughter, Adriana, sometimes acts as if she had not been affected by the feminist movement in the least.

She raises again in my mind the question of whether the so called feminine and masculine traits are inborn, or are brought out by the influence of a sexist society.

I don't mean that she is utterly feminine in the 19th Century sense of the word. She plays rough and takes no macho lip from her older brother, and if she were turned loose in a Sav-On drug store toy department, which I would not recommend, she would be just as likely to go for the boys' toys as for the girls' toys.

What I have in mind is her evidently inherent flair for the subtle intuitions, subterfuges, and ploys that in romantic fiction, at least, are associated with the *femme fatale.* It is possible, I suppose, that this talent was given to her in her genes; but perhaps she has learned it from watching the wrong kind of television.

One of the more spectacular demonstrations of her power over males, for it seems nothing less than that, was witnessed by her astonished father a year or so ago, when he walked down to the basement family room he had recently added to their house and found her dancing for the neighbor's smaller boys. She happens to be a serious interpretive dancer, in the tradition of Salome and Isadora Duncan. She has a gift for the dramatic posture and the passionate expression. When she raises her arms in supplication and rolls her eyeballs back in her head, so that only the whites show, she is devastating, and her act was much enhanced the day her father caught it by the fact that all her clothing lay in a heap on the floor. Her audience was entranced.

We went to Adriana's seventh birthday party Sunday afternoon and she seemed to have matured, as children often do, in the short time since we had seen her last. Of course birthdays always mature us, I suppose, reminding us of time's fleet passage. She had received a number of presents that seemed unisex enough, but her parents had refurbished her room as their present to her, and I suppose it could be called feminine, with white furniture and a wallpaper of pretty yellow flowers. My wife had given her a new quilted yellow bedspread and new yellow curtains, and they too, it seemed to me, were in the old-fashioned feminine vogue.

They hadn't been able to keep her from seeing the furniture before the party, but my wife had kept the curtains until the last minute, and they came to her as a surprise.

"How'd she like them?" I asked my wife, since I hadn't been there when they were presented.

"You know what she said? She said, 'Is that all there is?'"

"Don't worry," I said, "she'll remember those curtains years from now, when she's forgotten all the toys."

But I had already had my own disappointment, and couldn't feel too deeply for my wife. I had worn my new blue-seersucker suit and evidently neither of my daughters-in-law had even noticed it. I had wanted a seersucker suit since my high school days, but for one reason or another had never owned one. Then I had walked into Atkinson's a week or so earlier to buy a necktie, and saw the suit.

"It's your size," the young salesman said, "and affordable too."

I bought it, I am not vain about clothes, but I thought I would look nice in it at a party, and I wore it with a light blue classic Oxford cloth button-down shirt, blue knit tie, white belt, and white shoes. I felt as if I were back in the Summer of '39.

Of course it was my granddaughter's party, not mine, and the grandfather is not really a necessity on such occasions. I suppose I am something like Teddy Roosevelt in liking to be the center of attention. As his daughter Alice once said, "Daddy has to be the bridegroom at every wedding and the corpse at every funeral." I don't know why I expected to be adulated just because I had turned up in a suit that had been a staple of male attire since the 1890s, and whose main virtue was its understatement.

It wasn't until after dinner that I realized how mature and refined my granddaughter's instincts had become. Her mother had prepared a delicious French dinner of celery soup, chicken crepes and broccoli with cheese and bread crumbs, and we had all sat back from the table to enjoy the cake, and the last of the wine. Suddenly I sensed that my granddaughter was looking at me with that sustained concentration which is so exasperating in children. I was growing uneasy under this relentless scrutiny when she raised her eyes and purred, "Your new suit is *very* pretty."

"Why *thank* you," I said, surprised and extravagantly pleased. "You're the *only* one who noticed."

Though I am not given to demonstrations of emotion, I leaned toward her impulsively and gave her a kiss on the cheek, but I couldn't help suspecting, from her disingenuously innocent expression, that she had had one more lesson in how easy it is to handle men.

I don't understand why the feminists want to make boys and girls alike and deprive their own sex of all that power.

Grandpa, a Chip Off the Old Spock

Sunday, April 7, 1985

W E H A D T H E C A R E of our 2-year-old grandson over the weekend, and I was reminded of what it was like to have a small boy.

We had raised two, and it shouldn't have been much trouble for me.

He was supposed to be toilet trained, but there was always the chance of an accident. I told my wife I didn't remember much about what one did.

"Why should you?" she said. "You never did it."

I guess I was a lot like that character in Doonesbury. I did a lot of writing about what it was like to be a good father, and how it changed your life, but I never did much of the actual work.

I don't believe I even read Dr. Spock. But my wife did, and, in general, I agreed with his idea of not intimidating a child. I expected my boys to be prompt and literate and honest, but I didn't try to intimidate them, and I got two out of three. They aren't always perfectly prompt, but they do what they have to do, and that's what matters.

And they are literate and honest.

When my wife brought Trevor home Friday evening after work I was reading. The house had been utterly quiet. Everything in it deferred to the page before my eyes.

Suddenly there was a new presence. He is not a crybaby, or noisy, yet it was as if a chimpanzee had been let loose in the house. He demanded my attention. I had to watch him while my wife cooked dinner.

When he wanted to go out into the backyard to see the dog, I had to go with him. It would be too easy for him to run down to the pool. I had read too many stories, and written a few, about children drowning in backyard pools while their parents, or more often, their baby sitters, turned their backs "for just a minute."

I don't take much interest in children until they can talk well enough to ask intelligent questions; but I know that's short-sighted of me. At 2, of course, they are actually monsters, but, from a psychological point of view, quite interesting.

Trevor is clearly intelligent. He pronounces words very precisely, and speaks in sentences. When he tried to go outside by himself he came back to me and reported, "The door is locked."

What a miracle, I thought. Starting at zero, in two years he had learned to put an English sentence together—complete with noun, predicate and predicate adjective. An intellectual accomplishment of no small proportion. I wondered how long it had taken our species to develop language to that degree of complexity.

On the other hand, at the table he ate like a brute, slamming down his fork and spoon and picking his rice up in his hand and squeezing it into his mouth—what didn't fall on the floor.

If I remember correctly it took our sons years to learn proper table manners, and even today they aren't exquisite.

Sunday we drove to Bakersfield. My wife's brother and his wife were being given a surprise party on their 35th wedding anniversary by their son and daughter-in-law. It seems miraculous today not only that a husband and wife would stay together 35 years but also that their son and daughter-in-law would like them enough to want to help them celebrate.

It was a family reunion, and fortunately there were other small children. Trevor was dressed like a *boulevardier* in a striped

T-shirt with tan jacket and tan short pants and a tan bow tie (already the women in his life were teaching him to wear one). He is definitely a social animal and definitely, it gratified me to notice, heterosexual. He fastened onto a pretty little distant cousin of his in a pink dress and never gave her a moment's rest.

Well, there was *one* interruption in his amorous pursuit; when he forgot himself and wet his pants, which required my wife to come to the rescue. Fortunately, she had foreseen this contingency and had come equipped with an entirely new outfit that made him look like a railroad engineer. The little girl did not seem to be put off by his momentary embarrassment, and they were soon hard at their play again.

A relative of my wife's young niece had had some experience with children and big parties and had brought along a large trash bag full of toys, which soon were scattered all over the patio. I happened to be watching through a window while Trevor and his inamorata attacked a box that contained large plastic letters of the alphabet. Trevor started throwing them out of the box onto the patio deck with sweeping motions of his hand. The girl watched this vandalism for a moment, then joined in, picking up the remaining letters one by one and tossing them out. It was an all too prophetic scene, I thought. The innocent girl led into a wanton life by the boy she loves.

Trevor was so excited by this chance encounter that he stayed wide awake all the way back over the ridge to Los Angeles, while I had a hard time staying awake at the wheel.

My wife had decided to keep him another night, though he clearly told her, "I want to go home." Another perfect sentence. He cried, for the first time, when she tried to make him lie down. But he was exhausted, and soon fell asleep in spite of himself.

I think Dr. Spock would have been proud of me.

Scary Rides Knott His Cup of Tea

Monday, July 6, 1987

As a grown adult of refined tastes and uncertain health, I probably could have gone through the rest of my life without spending a day at Knott's Berry Farm.

However, having already survived Disneyland and Universal Studios, the other two great ornaments of our culture, I resigned myself to the third.

My wife and I went on a recent Sunday with three of our grandchildren—Adriana, 14; Alison, 10; and Trevor, 4.

I had been to Knott's Berry Farm in the late 1920s, when it was really a berry farm. You pulled off the road at an old farmhouse and went inside and had a piece of berry pie. You could also buy pies to take home. That was all.

No rides, no shows, no shooting galleries, no ghost towns, no fast-food stands, no lost-kids-information-booth, no first-aid station, no theater, no train.

It is now about the size of Monaco, and on Sundays has a greater population.

I was bewildered by the maze of streets and attractions, but with a map I oriented myself. After all, I was responsible for my party.

I was most worried about Trevor and myself. Being the youngest and the oldest, I felt we were the most vulnerable to fatigue, anxiety, sheer terror, and the necessity of going to the bathroom.

It turned out my granddaughters had come mainly to go on the scariest rides. I thought I might take the Soap Box Racer Ride with them, but a sign outside it warned:

"You must be in good health to take this roller-coaster type ride (free from heart and nervous disorders, weak back or neck, or other physical limitations)."

I failed on at least three counts—heart, back and other. I sat on a bench, watching the crowds stream by, while the girls went on the ride. My wife and Trevor went with them. I could hear their screams.

I think that those who sit on benches and watch the crowd go by see the best show. I found something encouraging in it. The '80s have been called the nasty decade, with everyone grubbing for himself in a selfish and uncivil society. I saw hundreds of young couples pushing strollers or carrying infants in their arms. One young woman stopped to change a diaper on a bench, doing it with the grace of a Degas figurine.

I don't think it was the low-key presence of security officers that accounted for the good-natured demeanor of the crowd. It seemed simply a kind of social decency, a willingness to live and let live; everyone seemed aware that everyone else was there for the same reason he was—to have a good time.

My wife and I wanted to go to the Good Time Theater to see the magic show, but the girls wanted to go on more rides. We split, and agreed to meet in a certain place an hour later.

I was not worried about the girls being alone in the crowd. I felt it was as safe as church.

We took Trevor to the magic show. He didn't like it when the magician did the old trick of cutting a girl in half. That always bothers me too; I'm always relieved when the girl jumps out.

When we met again the girls had been on the Corkscrew and two other rides of dubious advisability, but looked none the worse for it.

By this time everyone needed fodder. We grazed along, replenishing ourselves with a box of popcorn, a candied apple, an ice cream bar, a plate of cheese and chips, and five Pepsi Colas.

At 5 o'clock we lined up for the Dinosaur Ride. This is scary only if you're afraid of dinosaurs. It takes seven minutes. You get into a slowly moving car—they don't stop—and enter a maze of caves, going back through time to the Ice Age and then back into the Mesozoic Age of the dinosaurs. You pass a snarling saber-toothed tiger, a feeding giant tree sloth and a mammoth, and then come the dinosaurs.

A terrible tyrannosaurus rex rises on his hind legs, his forepaws uplifted, his ferocious maw agape; a horned stegosaurus feeds on a bank; an enormous brontosaurus drops his head down on its elongated neck as if to pick one of us from the car. Meanwhile, lightning flashes, and the cave is filled with an eerie screaming.

Trevor whimpered. It didn't do any good to tell him that all those beasts were extinct. After all, scientists don't know what caused the dinosaurs to disappear 60 million years ago—why should a 4-year-old kid believe they did?

We emerged into a world free of dinosaurs, but threatened with extinction by our own inventions.

The girls wanted to ride Montezooma's Revenge. This is a huge **U**-shaped track with a loop in the bottom of the cup. Your car goes through the loop, turning you upside down, then climbs one side of the **U**, then falls down backward, goes through the loop again, and goes backward up the other side of the **U**.

I didn't have to read the sign to see that it was not my cup of tea.

There was a 40-minute line. My wife and Trevor rode the Ferris wheel while I sat on a bench. I could see the top of Montezooma's Revenge and see the riders wave their arms on the backup and hear their screams.

I wondered if I had experienced my last thrill.

My wife drove us home over the freeway. I found out I had not experienced my last thrill.

The Rise and Fall of the Dodgers and Orioles

Sunday, July 13, 1986

I s a w my first T-ball game one recent Saturday morning out at Mar Vista Park on the Westside.

My grandson, Casey, was playing first base for the Orioles against the Dodgers.

If you are a baseball fan, a T-ball game may leave you in a state of permanent disorientation. Mere baseball will never seem the same again.

The players were mostly boys between the ages of 6 and 8. I believe the Dodgers had one girl; the Orioles were supposed to have one girl but she didn't show up.

I was reminded that at the ages of 6, 7 and 8, boys have not yet developed the athletic coordination that makes them so beautiful to watch at their games in later years. But now there is a kind of unvanquishable gallantry in their ineptitude.

And they are old enough that there is some sign of the grace that is to come; now and then a ball is struck cleanly, a fly is caught, a grounder is fielded—but mostly it is one catastrophe after another.

It is called T-ball because the ball is hit off a tee of adjustable height, so that it can be set to suit every batter. There is no pitching because few boys could hit a moving ball, and few could throw one across the plate with any consistency. Every at-bat would be a strikeout or a walk.

It was a pretty day; the sky was blue. A light breeze blew in the pine and eucalyptus trees. Mothers, fathers and siblings sunned in the bleachers along the first- and third-base lines. The Orioles wore orange, white and black; the Dodgers were in Dodger blue and white.

I tried to keep score. It wasn't easy.

A side is retired after three outs or after 10 men have batted, whichever comes first; it would take most of the day for a team to make three legitimate outs. Also, whenever the ball is thrown across home plate, all runners must stop where they are. Otherwise, the game would consist of continual scoring.

The Orioles were up first.

The first batter hit a slow roller to the pitcher. (Though the pitcher doesn't pitch, he still fields.) He bobbled the ball, kicked it and dropped it twice, by which time the runner had safely reached first. The pitcher threw the ball past home plate to interdict any further base running. Otherwise, the runner could easily have stolen all three remaining bases, since the fielders would never have been able to catch up with him.

The second batter hit a bouncer to the shortstop, who got in its way, knocked it down, fell to his knees, tried to pick it up, dribbled it away and finally trapped it in both hands, by which time, of course, the batter was rounding first and the first runner was rounding third. The shortstop alertly threw to home, thus stopping a run.

The third batter hit a Texas leaguer over second base, setting up a train of horrible sequences. The shortstop, the second baseman and the center fielder gave chase. Two of them bumped into each other and fell down. The third ran after the ball and fell on it. It squirted away. He scrambled to it, came up with it and tried to throw it home, but the ball merely rolled off his hand and fell about six feet toward second. Meanwhile, all three runners had scored.

Orioles 3, Dodgers o.

My grandson was up next. On his first swing he hit a high fly into right center field. The assorted fielders started after it like a pack of dogs chasing a fox. It came to a stop, and they fell on it like a football scrimmage line. Meanwhile, my grandson had run the bases for a clean home run.

Orioles 4, Dodgers o.

The next batter hit a roller to short. The shortstop bobbled the ball and finally got it in hand, but his throw to first was too short and too late. Runner safe.

The next batter hit a single to third.

The next batter hit a sharp grounder down the third-base line into left field for a home run.

Orioles 7, Dodgers o.

The next three batters all got to first base on infield errors, but the last one being the 10th batter the side was out, leaving the bases loaded.

The bottom half of the inning was pretty much like the top, except that my grandson caught a throw from the pitcher for the first clean putout of the game.

At the end of the inning I checked my score with the Orioles' assistant coach—a young woman named Cindy who carried a clipboard; she seemed to be in charge of the lineup and the batting order.

She confirmed my calculations that the score was Orioles 7, Dodgers 6.

There were two more innings. I gave up trying to keep score. My grandson made two more home runs for a perfect day at bat, and two more putouts.

"Do you realize," said my son, who was sitting with me, "that if he can do that 15 years from now, he'll be making a million dollars a year?"

At the end I checked again with Cindy. She said, "It was Orioles 21, and Dodgers either 19 or 20."

It may be too early, but if I were the Los Angeles Dodgers I'd get a scout out there.

Those kids play the Dodgers' kind of baseball.

CHAPTER 6

Pater of a Functional Family?

Grandpa Takes Potential Baseball Jock to Camp

Monday, July 27, 1987

OUR 8-YEAR-OLD grandson Casey stayed at our house a few days while he was attending the Manny Mota Baseball Camp at Scholl Canyon Playground, in the hills above Glendale.

He was my responsibility, man to man.

The camp started at 9 o'clock on a Monday morning. The playground has three baseball diamonds and a green field on a plateau high in the hills. It is surrounded by eucalyptus trees. To the south the spires of the downtown skyline arise from the smog.

We stood in line to register. There were about 30 boys. As they signed in, the man gave each a blue T-shirt with a picture of Manny Mota on it and the words "Manny Mota Baseball Camp."

A stocky man in T-shirt, shorts and a baseball cap gave a talk about the camp. He sounded sharp, firm and gentle. He said, "I'm Coach Paul," and, nodding toward a young man at his side, "this is Coach Gary."

Coach Paul said every boy would have to wear an athletic supporter and a cup, because of the danger of injury. "Not today," he said. "We'll take it easy today. But tomorrow."

The two coaches and two assistants led the boys out to the green field and formed them into two groups according to age: 7, 8, 9 and 10-year-olds; and 11-year-olds and older.

All of a sudden Manny Mota himself was standing out in front of them, like a knight in his white Dodger uniform with the big 11 on back. He gave them a talk.

Then the coaches lined them up and made them do calisthenics. This was the hard part. It reminded me of boot camp. The coach explained that the exercises were to limber them up so they wouldn't get hurt.

"What you learn here," he said, "will help you prevent injury all the way up to the pros."

It was out. The magic word. The impossible dream. The *pros*. There was always a chance. You might make it, even though the odds were about 50,000 to 1.

Coach Paul made them do two laps. They were soon straggled out with the little guys far in the rear.

Then the boys paired up and began playing catch with their partners. The older boys threw harder, faster, more accurately, and with the easy athletic grace that most boys achieve in their teens. Life is unfair.

Mota came off the field and slapped hands with the few parents who were still standing around. He had charisma, and he knew that it was important to spread it around.

Manuel Rafael Geronimo (Manny) Mota, out of Santo Domingo, played 20 years in the major leagues, 12 years with the Dodgers. Lifetime batting average .304. In three league championship series he got three pinch hits in five at-bats.

I went home, satisfied that my grandson was in good hands. I phoned his father and asked him if Casey had a jockstrap.

"A *jockstrap!*" He laughed. "Does he need one? I didn't have one until I was in high school."

I went to a Big 5 in Glendale and asked a young clerk if they had jockstraps. "I need a very small size," I said.

He raised an eyebrow.

"It's not for me," I said.

We picked out one, with plastic cup, that was labeled Young/Small.

I went back to the park about 2 o'clock. Casey's group was at batting practice, half lined up to bat, half out in the field with their gloves on. Casey was in line to bat. Coach Paul would toss the ball toward the plate from the side and the batter would swing at it. Sometimes he missed the ball entirely, just like Pedro Guerrero.

Casey came up. He swung at the first ball and missed. He swung again and missed. Manny Mota himself, now wearing a Manny Mota Baseball Camp T-shirt, walked over and moved Casey's feet. Just so. He told him how to hold the bat, how to keep his elbows in.

"Keep your eye on the ball!" he exhorted.

The next ball Casey belted over second base. He obviously had been metamorphosed by that laying on of hands.

Before dinner we played a game he had brought from home. It depended purely on luck and he beat me. "Haven't you got any games that require skill?" I asked.

He got a word game out of his satchel. It was a circular box in which nine letters were displayed at random. Each of us wrote down whatever words of four letters or more we could make of those nine letters.

The first group of letters was g, x, c, y, d, e, r, b, e. A few minutes later I had 10 words: bred, reed, deer, gyre, beer, cede, reedy, creed, dreg, breed. He had reed, deer and beer. He challenged gyre, cede, creed and dreg, but we looked them up in the dictionary and he conceded.

I think it's important to remind them that you know more than they do.

"How about Scrabble?" he said. I agreed. He won, 57-30.

When my wife came home I told her about the athletic supporter. "Do you want to show him how to put it on?" I asked.

"No," she said. "That's your job."

I asked him, "Do you know what a jockstrap is?"

He shook his head.

I told him what the jockstrap and the cup were for and how to put them on.

It was a rite of passage for us both.

Getting a Lock
on a Plumbing Problem

Tuesday, February 25, 1986

W E W E N T to our older son's house Saturday evening for his son Casey's seventh birthday party.

It turned out to be a situation comedy.

The best of seventh-birthday parties are slapstick affairs, but this one was disastrous.

Gail, our Italian daughter-in-law, cooked chicken cacciatore and zucchini sticks, which we ate with two bottles of champagne I had brought.

It was a happy family affair, with all five of our grandchildren present, along with their parents, and Gail's mother and her husband, and Gail's sister. It was a robust example of that vanishing phenomenon, the extended family.

The evening began to decline when I made my second trip to the bathroom. I noticed that the water level rose alarmingly when I flushed it, but then it subsided and I thought no more about it.

Half an hour later one of our granddaughters reported that the bathroom was flooded.

"Don't you have another bathroom?" I asked, knowing that a family of five could not very well get by with only one bathroom, although we had raised two boys with only one.

"It's flooded, too," she said. "I looked."

This news was no sooner delivered than Casey said he had to go. At once. He was told he would have to go outside, which he did with alacrity, evidently seeing some adventure in it.

The prospect did not seem so attractive to the rest of us.

My older son got a plunger and disappeared into one of the bathrooms. He came out, looking unsuccessful, and asked Gail if they had another plunger. She found one and he asked his younger brother to help him. They went into the separate bathrooms, each armed with a plunger. Great sucking and whooshing noises came from the bathrooms for several minutes. The two young men emerged defeated.

Meanwhile, my French daughter-in-law had had to go outside.

Our older son decided they would have to call a plumber, though it was Saturday night and they knew it would be expensive.

Gail began going through the Yellow Pages, trying to find a nearby plumber. She got an answer, explained the problem and asked for an estimate. It was $56 minimum, $88 if it took two men, plus 70 cents a foot beyond 80 feet of pipe. He said he could be there within half an hour.

Meanwhile, our younger granddaughter, Alison, discovered that she had locked herself out of her bedroom.

"How come her bedroom has a lock?" I asked innocently.

"To keep my *brothers* out," she explained.

The problem was that she had two keys, but she had inadvertently left both of them inside (she thought) and locked the door when she came out.

Our older son went into the hall to fiddle with the lock. He came out defeated.

Our older grandson decided to try picking it. "Has

anybody got a paper clip?" he asked. Evidently he had seen somebody pick a lock with a paper clip on TV. They are always picking locks on TV with paper clips or pen knives or credit cards. I happen to know it isn't that easy.

Somebody found a paper clip and we all went into the hall and watched while he picked at the lock. It wouldn't open.

Meanwhile the plumber came. He sized up the situation and said it would take two men. He said he'd wait outside in his truck for his partner to come. That might take 15 minutes.

Our older son got a screwdriver and a hammer and went to work on the lock. He took the handle and the face plate off and tried to open the lock by driving the screwdriver in with the hammer and twisting it. It wouldn't budge.

In his frustration he was pounding the hammer harder and harder, and I was afraid he would miss and hit his hand and the next thing we knew the paramedics would be crowding in.

The second plumber arrived and they came into the crowded hallway. One of the men left to get on the roof.

Our younger son took the screwdriver and the hammer and tried to drive the lock through the door by sheer physical force. He pounded and pounded but the lock held fast.

"You ought to write a testimonial for that lock," I said to our older son.

"It only cost about $10," he said.

Somebody said it was time to call a locksmith.

"And add another $50 to the bill?" he said. "I'll drill it."

He went out to the garage and got his electric drill and plugged it in and began to drill at the lock.

Meanwhile, the plumbers finished and Gail had to write a check for $88. They hadn't had to go beyond 80 feet.

Our son drilled holes through the two poles that held the lock, and finally the shell fell out in his hands, leaving the mechanism itself exposed. He simply inserted the screwdriver and turned it to the left and the door opened.

He held up the dismembered lock and said to his daughter, "This goes on display in your room."

She seemed more excited than dismayed by all the trouble she'd caused.

Of course he would have to buy a new lock, or at least a new door handle, and there would be some work to do with plastic wood around the door hole; but he had saved the price of a locksmith.

The next morning my son phoned to tell us that our granddaughter had found one of her keys outside the room.

Grandpas Are a Girl's Best Friend

Sunday, October 9, 1988

A L I S O N , my 11-year-old granddaughter, phoned the other day and said: "When are you going to take me to buy my earrings?"

She was calling in my IOU. Some months earlier, after a demoralizing resistance, her father had allowed her to have her earlobes pierced.

I had promised casually that I would take her out shopping for a pair of earrings.

Never having had a daughter, I am especially fascinated by my two granddaughters, though I wouldn't say that they yet hold me in mindless esteem or regard me as a fountain of wisdom.

Alison is petite, pretty and smart. She sometimes gives me intelligence tests, which I routinely fail. There's usually a trick to them, and its revelation makes me feel gullible as well as stupid.

I had renewed my promise to buy earrings for her several times, but I had never delivered. Now she had me nailed to the wall. I promised to pick her up at home one day at 3:30 p.m.

When I arrived, she was ready. Her mother suggested that we go to the shopping center at Pico and Westwood. "Don't buy anything too gaudy," her mother said. "We don't want her to look like a harlot."

We drove to the mall. When we walked inside, we were swallowed up in a seemingly endless cornucopia of goods.

We passed a jewelry shop and stopped to study the merchandise in the display windows. A pair of diamond earrings caught my eye.

They were hardly a quarter-inch in diameter. Not too big, I thought. I turned my head to read the little price card. It said $3,250.

"Those are a bit expensive," I said. She nodded silently. I was glad she agreed.

"Let's try the May Co.," I said. It was down at the end of the mall, about two blocks away.

In the May Co., we walked through the cosmetics section, with its ambiance of seductive perfumes. The jewelry section was nearby. Dozens of earrings were displayed in glass cases and on open tables.

I saw a pair in a glass case that seemed modest enough. They were tiny gold hearts with one tiny pearl in each. They were only $24.95. "How do you like those?" I asked her.

"I like them," she said, not going into ecstasies. She turned around to an open table behind her. "I like those, too," she said.

She pointed to a pair that looked to me exactly like the diamonds at the jewelry store. They were round and sparkly, cut like diamonds; but they were zircons and only $14.95.

"They're certainly a lot cheaper than the diamonds," I said, realizing that I was being swayed by purely monetary values.

They were cheaper than the hearts, too.

"Would you rather have the hearts?" I asked magnanimously. "I like them," she said without great enthusiasm, "but I like these, too," turning back to the zircons. She knew what she wanted.

We took the zircons. I began looking for an ice cream parlor, thinking that a little tete-a-tete over ice cream would be pleasant. "I know where one is," she said.

We got into the car and she directed me to a Penguins parlor about two miles away.

It's amazing how quickly they learn their neighborhoods.

"It's not really an ice cream parlor," she said as I parked in the mini-mall. "They sell yogurt, not ice cream."

I do not love yogurt. But, as Johnny Carson said, "it's the only live culture we have in Los Angeles."

We both ordered medium-size dishes at $1.39 each and sat in the parlor, spooning them up in amiable silence. It wasn't half bad.

When we got back to her house, she opened the jewelry box and showed her mother the earrings. I was rather startled at how dazzling they seemed. Her mother looked me in the eye. I saw her dismay. I knew what she was thinking.

"Oh well," her mother said. "Maybe she can wear them on special occasions."

In a minute, Alison had taken the earrings and put them on. She looked sensational.

What's a grandfather for?

The Eyes Have It
for the Young Soldier

Monday, March 9, 1992

M Y   W I F E   A N D   I went to Georgia a weekend ago for a rite of passage.

Our grandson Chris, 21, was graduating after 16 arduous weeks of basic infantry training at Ft. Benning, and we wouldn't have missed it.

We went with his parents, our son Doug and daughter-in-law Jacqueline. We flew together to Atlanta, rented a car and drove to the Hilton Columbus in Columbus, six miles from the fort. The hotel is charming. It is built on the site of a Civil War warehouse and employs some of its original bricks. At dinner we learned that Georgians talk different. They do not say "you all," as I supposed, nor even "y'all." They say "yaw." "Yaw enjoy your dinner now."

The ceremony was to start at 9 o'clock the next morning. The fort lies on green rolling hills surrounded by piney woods. Fortunately, we arrived early. We parked and were standing on a hill above the assembly hall when we heard a distant chorus of male voices chanting in cadence. It was thrilling.

Soon a company of soldiers in dress greens topped a rise, marching in ranks. Their shoes fell on the road in rhythm with their chant. They sang:

I got a letter in the mail
Go to war; go to jail;
And it won't be long 'til I get back home.
Mama don't you cry.

Your little boy ain't gonna die.

The company marched past us, eyes straight ahead, arms and legs swinging in unison.

Another chorus sounded in the distance and soon another company appeared in the road and marched toward us. As it neared, we saw our man, on the edge of a rank. He grinned. His eyes moved briefly toward us.

As an ex-Marine I was shocked. If only slightly, he had broken ranks. Thank God his drill instructor, marching to the left of the front rank, had not noticed.

The hall was crowded with relatives and friends. The two graduating companies were seated up front in the wings. We made eye contact with Chris again, and this time he smiled and waved with impunity.

The fort band was at the back, blasting out military marches. We stood for the "Star-Spangled Banner" and the invocation. A colonel talked briefly, a French liaison officer made a speech about brotherhood. Now and then the soldiers would express their approval or disapproval by barking—one short bleat, in unison.

Afterward we met Chris briefly outside and then followed him back to his barracks. His comrades were packing their bags for their various assignments. Chris told us he had been assigned to Panama, and had to leave that afternoon. His mother was dismayed. Panama seemed like the end of the world to her. Besides, she had hoped he would be able to spend two days with us.

We drove him into town for lunch, then took him to the hotel, where we had adjoining rooms. He was repentant over his lapse of discipline. "When I saw you I just couldn't help it," he said. "If the DI had seen me I'd be doing pushups for a week."

We reminded him that he was through with his DI forever.

He was going to a new world. He was a soldier, not a boot. He said he had to repack his bag. He dumped everything on the floor, including four camouflage uniforms. He said he had to get one pressed. The hotel didn't do pressing, but they said they could send up an ironing board and iron, which they did. My wife wound up ironing the young man's uniform. She is an expert.

He had to be at the airport at 4 o'clock. He was flying to Charleston at 4:30 and on to Panama at midnight. The Army doesn't fool around. Only two other men from his company had been assigned to Panama. It was not regarded as easy duty.

We said our goodbys and watched him vanish into the boarding tunnel. He had had his troubles as a teen-ager. But he had a sense of honor and a sense of humor. In a recent letter to us he had griped about the hardships and humiliations of basic training, as all soldiers do: "It's been one hell of a 16 weeks here, but then I wasn't going to straighten out my life overnight. I've learned here to appreciate the values that freedom carries. And it feels good to know that I'm able to contribute to keeping this country free."

We waited in the terminal, looking out the window, as the plane taxied to the end of the runway, turned, and took off. We watched it rising into the sky and vanishing over the horizon.

We knew, as the Army says, that he was going to be all that he can be.

One Day in the Lice of a Soldier

Monday, November 15, 1993

ARMY LIFE is no bed of roses. My grandson, Chris, a specialist with an infantry battalion in Panama, sent his parents the following letter.

I do not often turn this space over to someone else's prose, but I think his letter is so graphic, so vivid, so hilarious in its anguish, that it deserves publication.

"Dear Family:

"Well, we just came back from the jungle and we're planning to move out again in two days.... First let me tell you about this last week, which was perhaps the worst and most miserable field mission that I've been on since I've been in Panama.

"I tell you, they're trying to kill me before I go home. The first five days we spent building a phony village for another company to assault, while at the same time the other company built a village for us to assault.... In wartime an attack element never gets to see what they're going to attack.

"Anyway, we worked from dawn to dark using plywood and two-by-fours to build all kinds of huts and towers, a mess hall, hospital, barracks and a 20-foot water tower.

"Our squad had to dig seven foxholes, and I spent many back-breaking hours digging under an intense sun. By the end of the first day, I was sunburned and very dehydrated.

"At night a storm came in, and it rained all night. We were soaked, muddy and miserable. The mosquitoes and chiggers were biting constantly.

"We had very little sleep, and each morning we were up at 0500 hours, infested with bites from head to toe. Everyone was in a bad mood and all the sergeants were yelling and giving commands, which seemed to irritate us more.

"Finally at the end of the week, we were done and it was time to start the mission. I was beat. Everyone was beat but we had to continue. There was no choice. We were trucked over to the area and began to prepare for the assault...the next morning.

"But when morning came there was a small problem. The platoon medic discovered lice on one of the soldiers. After checking other soldiers, he realized that the whole platoon had lice, including me. Eventually it was confirmed that the whole company had lice.

"The Army does not mess around with lice. The medics demanded that the entire company be sent out of the field to be properly treated. The big commanders were against this because they believe in mission first, welfare second, a policy that has won all our wars. But what a medic says must go...."

The letter goes on to explain that helicopters were supposed to take the soldiers back to their base, but the choppers didn't show up.

"It rained all night. We were wet, muddy, cold and infested with lice. I wanted to curl up in a little ball and die."

Chris wrote that finally it was decided that if everyone had lice there was no one left to get them. So they went ahead with the assault.

"We began our march through the jungle. I was completely burned out of energy. It was just one tall mountain after another. My legs were giving out on me. I looked like a big mud ball with a rifle.

"Finally we reached the objective, and I was picked to be the first man to enter the line. My job was to clean up the wire that surrounded the village and shout at the enemy while the engineers crawled up and placed C4 explosives under the wire to blow it up.

"When the C4 blew up, a big space was left in the wire, and the company started filing through to assault the objective. Everybody threw smoke grenades to conceal us. The smoke got so thick that everybody started to get lost. Also we started to choke and gag. There was the sound of blank gunfire in every direction. I didn't know which way was which....

"Finally I found an open clearing and ran to fresh air. I located the 60 gunner and ran to his position. He was cussing because his gun was jammed. I assessed the situation and ran ahead, telling him to follow me, but he just sat there trying to fix his gun. When he finally fixed it he was so happy he started firing it right away and didn't notice me about 20 meters away. So the asshole killed me."

Being theoretically dead didn't excuse Chris from making the 10-mile march to the trucks for the ride to home base. Then he and all the men spent a wretched day being deloused.

The young man isn't complaining, understand. He's just giving us a graphic account of what his life in the Army is like. Underneath the misery we can sense the pride.

We're proud of him, and we're glad to know that he's deloused.

Casey at Bat at the Ol' Ball Game

Monday, July 25, 1994

N O T   A L L   teen-age boys are out on the streets defiling garage doors, robbing markets and shooting one another. Some of them are expending their energies on the great American pastime of baseball.

My wife and I drove out to Santa Monica High School the

other day to watch our grandson Casey in a game between Samohi and the Brentwood Eagles Baseball Club. It was a summer school game played mostly for practice and coaching, no league standings involved.

It was a workday and few spectators were in the bleachers. Our older son, Curt, and his wife, Gail, were among them, Casey being their son. Also Casey's younger brother, Trevor, was with us. Peter O'Malley, owner of the Dodgers, was there in a business suit. His son, Brian, was playing left field, right next to Casey, at center field.

Ocean breezes blew across the grass field, making the day surprisingly cool. A row of slender eucalyptus lined the outfield, and beyond it stood a large hotel. The Santa Monica skyline rose in the distance.

Casey came up to bat just after we arrived. He is a strong kid; works out with barbells. But the Santa Monica pitcher was too big and too good. He blew him away with three quick strikes.

As the game progressed Casey redeemed himself with catches of deep hit balls and fine throws to the infield. Then he struck out again. The game went only seven innings, Santa Monica winning 3-1.

After the game, the teams shook hands in a ritual that has been in dispute in some high schools, but which to me seemed gentlemanly and mature, and rather beautiful to watch.

There was one exciting play when a Santa Monica batter hit a fly deep to left center. Brian tried to scoop it off the ground and flubbed it. Casey picked it up and threw to second, probably cutting off a run. I know what happened because O'Malley told me. He has a good eye for baseball.

Probably not one member of those teams will make it in the major leagues, but who knows? Maybe Casey will be the next Mike Piazza, if he learns to hit.

Meanwhile they were all good-looking boys in their uniforms and batting helmets, and they were there to play, not to plunder. The only gangs they belonged to were their teams.

Our plan was to have a family dinner at Marie Callender's on National Boulevard where my granddaughter, Alison, recently began work as a waitress. She is trying to earn money for college.

Casey couldn't go. He said he had to do homework. Can you believe it?

Our granddaughter had the maitre d' seat us at a table where she could wait on us. I was eager to see how she handled a rather gauche crowd like us—her mother and father, her grandparents and 11-year-old Trevor, who is rather uncivilized.

She was fine. Patient, quick, pleasant and pretty. The first thing I did was ask for a vodka tonic. "We don't serve alcohol," she informed me sweetly.

But I was in a good mood. After the game, we had stopped by Curt and Gail's house in Mar Vista and found they didn't have any vodka, which meant I would have to go without my usual evening fix. It has become an inflexible family ritual that my wife fixes me a vodka tonic—one—each evening before dinner, and has one herself. This is usually followed by dinner and a sex-and-violence movie. Such is culture in today's world.

When we found the cupboard bare, my wife volunteered to drive to the market and pick up a bottle of vodka, a gesture that I took as a recognition of my patience and civility. So I had my fix after all.

Earlier in the week, Gail and our other grandson, Chris, son of Doug and Jackie, came over to our house to take me swimming. I had not been in our beautiful pool once this summer, because of my difficulty in managing the steps.

Being a physical therapist, Gail knew how to get me into

the water using a walker. It was a tedious business, but it worked. I had a good swim, but Gail's presence probably kept me from drowning.

Chris was recently discharged after two years in the Army, mostly in the jungles of Panama. He has developed a manly physique, which he improves by workouts at a Pasadena gym. Thus I, the paterfamilias, am surrounded and supported by exemplary grandchildren. The word *family* never seems to be used in a positive sense anymore, but I would say we are a functional one.

Of course, I never could hit.

CHAPTER 7

Eternal Vexations and Other Gripes

He Pants to Get on Best-Dressed List

Sunday, January 17, 1988

ONCE AGAIN I have been overlooked in the Tailors Council of America's annual list of America's 10 best-dressed men.

I don't know what I have to do to please those people.

One of the problems, I suspect, is that the Tailors Council is composed entirely of men, and that they do not see the best-dressed men with a woman's eye for style.

Most men I know dress for women and couldn't care less what the Tailors Council thinks.

Also, I suspect, the tailors tend to be swayed by the price tag on a man's clothes and vote accordingly. What is especially perceptive, for example, in naming Lee Iacocca the best-dressed man in industry? Iacocca always looks neat, I admit, but if I had his money to spend on clothes, I could look neat, too.

Why is Senator Bob Dole the best-dressed man in government? If they wanted to be creative, they could have named Lt. Col. Oliver North. He really looked sharp in his Marine Corps greens.

I have always suspected that in the past the council has avoided naming me by leaving out the media as a category. But this time the media were included, and Ted Koppel was named best-dressed man.

I have no quarrel with the way Koppel dresses, but we never see him except when he's dressed for TV. Did they ever catch him on a weekend at home? How does he look when he's feeding the dog or driving down to the store for a six-pack?

This year the tailors named Cary Grant as the best-dressed

man in motion pictures. That seems spooky to me. They excused themselves by noting that "the selection of Cary Grant was necessitated due to the lack of any current actor who sartorially represents the motion picture industry."

They point out that Grant's collars, which were always "just right," and "the length of the sleeve, too, just correctly showing the cuff of the shirt...."

I admit that Grant was a classy dresser, but if they're going to let the departed in, where does it stop? Will Teddy Roosevelt be next?

Maybe my problem is that this year I changed from a 15 collar, which I have worn most of my adult life, to a 15½. I just got tired of being choked. The result is a space between my neck and my collar, but I'm sure the tailors will agree that comfort is half of style.

Also, although I have always resented them, I bought a dozen of those so-called European-size shirts that don't have sleeve lengths in full and half sizes. Instead, they come 32-33 or 34-35. I bought half a dozen of each. Since I'm a perfect 33½, my sleeves are now either one inch too long or one inch too short. If Iacocca bought a dozen shirts that didn't fit, he'd give them away.

I thought this might be my year, if only because of the two jackets my wife bought me by mail order.

One is a loose-hanging gray cotton jacket with big pockets. She bought me two T-shirts to go with it—one blue and one cerise. When I wore the jacket to the office with the cerise T-shirt, it provoked a lot of comment.

"Hey, you look like Don Johnson," one woman said.

I do believe I looked at least as good as Koppel.

The other jacket she bought me is pink silk. It has a rough weave and has the virtue of looking pink in the sunlight and beige under artificial light. When I go to indoor-outdoor parties in the afternoon, I'm a chameleon.

How many men did the tailors see this year with jackets that can do that?

The tailors say they favor the "two-styled look—one for dress and business, and the other for the relaxed activities and weekends...."

They probably checked me out on a weekend when I was wearing my old red plaid shirt, a pair of blue jeans, one of my sailing caps and my boat shoes.

The tailors may not know it, but old plaid shirts and blue jeans are the weekend outfit favored by most stylish American males.

As far as I'm concerned, the tailors can consider me out of the running.

I recognize prejudice when I see it, and I'm not going back to Size 15 collars just to be picked as one of America's 10 best-dressed men. Maybe, like Cary Grant, I'll get my recognition when I'm gone.

Getting a Charge Out of Aerobics

Sunday, October 20, 1985

I'VE FINALLY got in on a fad.

I'm into aerobics.

At least, I think it's aerobics.

Three mornings a week, at 8 o'clock, I pump a stationary bicycle 20 minutes, work with light arm and leg weights, and row a rowing machine for 20 minutes at the Pasadena Athletic Club.

Health clubs are a vogue in Southern California. Some of them are built in the style of ancient Roman baths, with opulent pools and steam rooms and marble statues of the gods; others appear overnight in storefronts, so that anyone passing by can see dozens of beautiful young people inside, working out with what has always seemed to me a ludicrous waste of energy. Of course, I suppose one sex meets another at these clubs, and their energies are soon enough put to more pleasantly sensuous occupations.

It wasn't pleasantly sensuous occupations I had in mind when I joined the Pasadena Athletic Club. I merely hoped to get my pump, pipes and valves into reasonably good condition so that I could go on pursuing the purpose of life, which is to keep on living and see what happens next.

But I expected exercising at the club to be a bore, even though the exercise room has a great window overlooking the San Gabriel Mountains, which are often quite beautiful in the morning.

The club is not a typical youth health club, with muscular young men and supple young women sweating foolishly to improve perfection. Most of us are older; some are even older than I am, but there are enough youngsters to remind us of our youth.

Thanks to modern technology, the bicycles are equipped with tiny television screens between the handlebars. I immediately acquired a set of headphones, and I now watch NBC's Today show, keeping up with every day's fresh disasters.

But the rowing machine was sheer boredom. I tried to imagine that I was rowing the Hellespont or some such challenge. Nothing worked. It was a long 20 minutes.

Then one day, a young man took the machine beside mine. He was wearing a headset that was attached to some kind of player in a bag. He looked exalted.

He noticed my envy and put the headphones on my head. I was at once drowned in sound—enveloping, flawless, magnificent sound. It was Beethoven's Seventh. It couldn't have sounded any better to the conductor himself.

"It's a laser disc," the young man told me. He opened the player and showed me a silver disk four or five inches in diameter. "No scratches," he said. "Lasts forever."

The next day he let me listen again. "This is *great* rowing music," he said.

It was Vivaldi. "The Four Seasons."

That night I told my wife about the wonderful machine that took the boredom out of rowing. A week later she came home with one—everything except the batteries.

I bought six rechargeable batteries and put them in and tried to play Beethoven's "Moonlight Sonata." Nothing. No spin. No sound.

Finally I called my older son, who was a radio repairman in the Air Force and knows electronics. He suggested that I first try *charging* the batteries.

I hooked up the charging unit to the wall plug in our living room and an hour later went to bed. In the morning I tried the player. I was rewarded by the mellow notes of the famous sonata. Jubilantly, I set out for the club. When it came time to row, I put the earphones on and turned on the player. It was magnificent. For three minutes. And then it stopped.

I was crushed. I went on rowing the Hellespont without music.

When I got home, I automatically flipped on the switch that controls all the power outlets in the living room. Suddenly, I knew what was wrong. The night before, after I had gone to bed, my wife had flipped the switch off, cutting off the power to my battery pack. It had charged for less than an hour.

I now have it charging for 15 hours, and I look forward to the bliss of rowing to the "Moonlight Sonata."

I plan to get "Beethoven's Ninth," so I can hear that glorious "Ode to Joy" while I row.

I expect it will be almost as good as being young.

She Loves Travel, He Thinks It Sphinx

Sunday, December 10, 1989

M Y A N X I E T Y about going to Egypt with a Music Center group next spring has been deepened by messages from two distinguished correspondents.

As I said recently, I am not an enthusiastic traveler; I am bored by airports, uneasy in airplanes, fatigued by luggage, frustrated by foreign languages and poisoned by strange foods.

My wife, on the other hand, is an energetic traveler; she would be at home in the headwaters of the Amazon or in Stone Age New Guinea. In fact, I am surprised that she has not dragged me to those two places.

It isn't that I don't want to see Egypt. The pyramids and the Sphinx are among the great monuments of the world. But I have heard hideous stories about the heat, the insects, the din and the congestion of Cairo. (Some say it is worse than Los Angeles.)

One of my correspondents, Charlton Heston, notes that, like my wife, his wife loves to travel. "So does my daughter, my daughter-in-law and my mother, who is somewhere in her late 80s. So does my assistant and just about all the women I know (a pretty short list, actually). Any one of them will happily whip off to anywhere from Khartoum to Kennebunkport on a moment's notice...."

Being bolder than I would care to be, Heston says: "I think

it's a sexual difference. (There aren't supposed to *be* any sexual differences now, but you and I know better.) Women are nest-builders, they can build one anywhere. Men are territorial; they want to walk barefoot on land they've marked as theirs, through the seasons."

As an actor, though, Heston makes about half his living on the road. "Most of the things I like to do and most of the people I like to see are available on the ridge we built our house across (in Coldwater Canyon). My wife, though, like yours, is tireless in her determination to explore the world."

He encloses a travel story on Egypt written by his wife, Lydia Clarke Heston, for The Times. Despite the inconveniences she describes, the tone is romantic: "Our old haunts in Luxor and the Valley of the Kings, to our relief, were unchanged, even more romantic with magical, purple twilight and the same open, friendly faces of village people everywhere...."

Heston concludes: "You should see the pyramids before they're gone.... Go answer the riddle of the Sphinx."

The distinguished Norman Cousins writes: "Your lamentations about travel are not idiosyncratic. At one time, the main concern had to be over assaults on one's intestinal flora and the insistencies they imposed on the daily agenda. But these penalties now take second place to the ordeals of the airport—the distance from the sidewalk to the departure gate; the long line at the check-in counter; the uncertainty represented by overbooked flights; the cosmic distance to connecting planes; the delays...."

"Worse still is the torment of the crowded freeway en route to the airport. This experience becomes particularly obnoxious when you discover on arrival that the flight was canceled...."

Cousins also discloses that his wife is devoted to travel, like my wife and Heston's: "Like Denise, Ellen has a yen for

Florence and Venice and other exotic places. Like you, my desires in these directions are not unquenchable. The most important thing we have in common, of course, is that our wives have put up with us in these and other respects for half a century."

But how can we go to Egypt in the spring when we're going to be remodeling our house?

Don't Eat if You Know
What's Good for You

Monday, June 15, 1992

A s o n e who has reached the age in which prolonging one's life seems a primary concern, I am exasperated by the vacillation of medical authorities on just what will do that and what won't.

I grew up believing, as I was told, that if I ate my vegetables and drank milk every day I would be strong and healthy. I have been healthy most of my life although as a boy I ate a Snickers almost every day, and since achieving manhood I have probably drunk more than one beer every day.

Lately, however, I have read that too much milk is not good for you, and on the other hand, beer in moderate amounts will make you not only healthier but also happier.

In recent years I have almost given up beer for wine, which I drink almost every day. That change came after I read in the paper that the French have fewer heart attacks than we do because they drink a lot of wine. On the other hand, I have read that the Japanese have fewer heart attacks because they eat a lot of rice. I do not like rice and I am not going to eat it in large amounts to avoid a heart attack. Wine, OK; rice, no.

Recently the brilliant medical essayist Lewis Thomas said that television has reduced the rate of heart attacks in America. That's because television advertises all kinds of medicines that contain aspirin, which is said to have a salutary effect on the cardiovascular system. I'd take an aspirin every day but I'm told it abrades the stomach.

If you read the medical news in the paper thoroughly, as I used to, you can find a lot of curious theories, based on scientific research, that almost everything they once thought was good for you is actually bad for you, and vice versa.

For the past several years I have been strung out by the controversy over cholesterol. I don't even know for sure what cholesterol is (I think it's waxy), but for many years, from reading the paper, I believed that it was bad for you.

I took to avoiding cholesterol whenever I could. Our refrigerator is crammed to this day with products whose labels testify to their freedom from it, or at least to its minuscule presence.

Now I have recently read in the paper about new findings that the absence of cholesterol can give you profound psychic problems. "These studies throw into a cocked hat the whole proposition that every American should lower his cholesterol level," said a scientist involved in this latest discovery.

The psychic problems may include personality changes so severe that they can even lead to violent death by causing anger, irritability, aggressiveness and increased risk-taking, including suicide.

In other words, if you don't get your cholesterol, you can go crazy.

On the other hand, these experts say, if you have any kind of heart trouble, you have to cut down on cholesterol or it may kill you.

I have reached the point where I am not going to worry about what I ought to ingest to prolong my life. I am beginning to question all the accepted rules. As I have previously noted, I recently had lunch with a retired colleague who looked extremely fit. I asked him what he was doing to maintain his health. He said he had asked his doctor what difference it would make if he gave up fats, sweets, alcohol and red meat. The doctor said, "It will probably add three months to your life."

He and I agreed that those last three months would probably not be too much fun anyway, so why give up what you enjoy merely to live three miserable months longer?

I also read recently that every step you climb will add eight seconds to your life. I used to take the elevator up one floor at The Times (27 steps) to reach the garage level. I began climbing the steps instead of taking the elevator. Then I figured that if I climbed one flight every weekday for a 50-week year, that would add 56,160 seconds, or 936 minutes, or 15 hours to my life.

I decided that adding 15 hours to my life was not worth having to climb 6,750 steps. I decided to throw those hours in with the three months I might add by giving up everything I enjoy eating and drinking. (The question now is moot because I no longer go into The Times every day.)

From now on I'm not reading any of the medical news. Like the French, I'm just going to go on drinking wine and taking one day at a time. I believe our reason for being here is to stay alive, enjoy and see what happens next.

As for cholesterol, I'm keeping it low; I'd rather be crazy than dead.

Nose Has Him Beating
Around the Bush

Monday, March 18, 1991

I SUPPOSE I'm going to have to say what happened to my nose.

The damage isn't going to go away in a few days, and already I have been besieged by questions.

"Whadja do t'yur nose?" There have been several variations, some of them humorous and some rude.

Obviously, there is going to be no end to it, and I might as well try to forestall this barrage by telling the true story.

What we are talking about is a large scab on the bridge of my nose from the eyes to the knob, or whatever it's called. My nose, in fact, was skinned, or gouged, as if with a scraper, for almost its entire length. For several days it was a raw wound, but fortunately it has scabbed over. It is still disgusting but not shocking.

I can't blame people for being curious. It is bound to excite curiosity. It is a strange wound. Some people politely pretend to ignore it, but they can't hide their curiosity.

I can hear them asking themselves, "How the *hell* did he do that?"

It is not bashed. It is not broken. Actually, the best word to describe it is *gouged*.

I remember when I was a kid I broke an arm at school on the horizontal bar and it was put in a cast. I got so tired of the same old question—"Whadja do t'yur arm?"—that I began lying, just to amuse myself. I worked up a repertoire of improbable explanations that were almost always accepted as gospel. That taught me that people will believe almost anything but the truth.

Several times when people have asked me "Whadja do t'yur nose?" I have answered, "My wife hit me."

To my embarrassment they believed me. Well, why not? It was simple and direct, and I imagine that most people assumed that she had reason.

I'm not saying she doesn't often have reason, but people who know her know she would not strike me. Or most of them do. Or do they? How can I be so sure myself?

She can be a spitfire, but so far she has never used violence on me. Of course that may be because she would feel that she was abusing her physical inferior.

I have thought of saying I was drunk and ran into a concrete abutment. It might be plausible enough, but my wound does not fit with that kind of accident.

I might say that I was playing baseball with my grandchildren and the ball hit me in the nose. However, it is well known that I no longer engage in sports, even with my grandchildren, and, again, a baseball would tend to flatten one's nose, not scrape or gouge it.

So there is, finally, nothing to do but tell the truth. I am aware that the truth may be harder to believe than any of the previous fabrications.

First, I must explain that I wear a pair of steel-rimmed eyeglasses.

I have never worn steel-rimmed glasses before; they were for older people. But the optometrist assured me they were not too old for me. He told me they were called Bushes because they were like those worn by President Bush. I did not vote for Bush, but I thought—what the heck—it wouldn't hurt to wear glasses like those worn by the President of the United States.

One feature of the glasses is that the bridge is a thin steel bar curved like a scimitar. It is, in fact, a deadly weapon.

Now we come to the part of the story that may be hard to believe. I was standing in my bedroom trying to get into my shorts. I was standing on my left leg and trying to work my right leg through the right leg of my shorts. I am not a stork. I lost my balance, which I have a tendency to do.

You may wonder why I was wearing my glasses while putting on my shorts. I do not see too well, and my glasses are the second thing I put on after showering. I put my T-shirt on first so I won't have to pull it over my glasses.

The rest is simple. I pitched to the floor like a board, face first, into the rug. My glasses were shoved down the length of my nose by the force of my fall, gouging the flesh like a snowplow.

At my cry, my wife came to my assistance. She washed my nose and applied a bandage and cleaned up the blood in the rug.

That's my story. If you don't believe it, you can believe any other story you like. I realize other stories may sound a lot more probable.

I'll tell you one thing: I've bought my last pair of Bush glasses.

Where Have All the Doctors Gone?

Sunday, March 2, 1986

I AM NOT a hypochondriac, but as I grow older, I become more susceptible to intimations of mortality, and to fortify myself as long as possible against its inevitable due date, I keep trying to collect a medical team.

I had, at one time, an internist, a dermatologist, a periodontist, a cardiologist, an ophthalmologist, a urologist and an ear, nose and throat man.

I have found each of these necessary to keep the parts working until, like the one-horse shay, everything wears out simultaneously.

The trouble with this plan is that doctors are not (as we tend to think of them) immune to physical and psychological breakdowns themselves. Consequently, my doctors keep dying on me, or going away, or retiring, or becoming otherwise unavailable.

To begin with, the captain of my team, so to speak, was the eminent Dr. Edgar F. Mauer, a neighbor of ours on Mt. Washington and my personal physician for more than 30 years. I used to refer to Dr. Mauer as Dr. Reap, but now that he has retired, I see no reason for shielding him any longer from public knowledge of his idiosyncrasies.

Dr. Mauer was widely respected in the profession as a diagnostician. I remember a heroic diagnosis he made once of an ailment of mine. I had a terrible pain in my neck and had gone to an orthopedist, who told me I had a spinal-disk injury and put me in a sort of canvas noose from which I was to hang for half an hour twice a day. It went around my head and under my chin and was suspended in a doorway. When my wife came home and for the first time saw me hanging in the kitchen doorway, she shrieked.

Since hanging in suspension did nothing to relieve the pain, I went to Dr. Mauer. He asked me dozens of questions and seemed to be stumped until I added, as an afterthought, that it hurt in the front.

"In the *front!*" he exclaimed. "Why didn't you say so? I thought it hurt in the *back*."

Dr. Mauer called in a colleague and told him my symptoms. "Remember the case we had like this?" he asked.

His colleague nodded. "Thyroiditis."

"You remember what the treatment was?"

"Aspirin," his colleague said.

I believe that may have been the only time in medical history that a distinguished physician, in consultation with a colleague, recommended aspirin as a specific for a serious ailment.

I was saved.

Since Dr. Mauer retired, to sit up in his aerie on top of the hill reading Mencken, Sassoon, Norman Douglas and Max Beerbohm, I have found another general practitioner, a pupil of Dr. Mauer's, whom I like and trust.

But my dermatologist retired because he could no longer cope with the paper work demanded in modern medical practice.

My ophthalmologist retired just the other day to write his memoirs.

My urologist retired, and my ear, nose and throat man is already the dean in his field and may retire any day.

Let me tell you about my periodontists. The first one died suddenly of a heart attack in his 50s. He had been a nut on eliminating sweets and alcohol. As a result of his preaching, I have rarely eaten sweets ever since.

When he died, I found a periodontist who did good work, but he hated The Times and never failed to vilify it when he had me in his chair. I didn't mind his not liking The Times, but I couldn't stand being harangued about it when he had me down with my mouth open and full of cotton wadding.

I found a younger periodontist who did not seem to be enraged by The Times. I found out that he read no newspapers at all.

"I get all the news I need listening to my car radio on the way to work," he said.

I drifted away. I could not stand to have my teeth worked on by a man who didn't read a newspaper at all.

I found another man who seemed ideal. He was a tough old bird, about my age, who had been a dentist with the 8th Air Force in World War II. Then he took a round-the-world tour, found out he liked the Philippines, and stayed there to open up a clinic.

My next periodontist was a relatively young man, in his 40s. He was an artist. The best I'd ever found. I told him about my doctors leaving me.

"Don't worry," he said. "I'll outlive you."

Then he fell from a ladder in his basement at home and suffered a severe leg injury that forced him into early retirement.

I am now going to a very young man who seems competent and amiable; I wish him good health.

And I pray for my cardiologist.

CHAPTER 8

Some of the Words I Live By

Is That All There Is to a Lifetime?

Sunday, May 21, 1989

THERE HAS BEEN much speculation on the meaning of life. Why are we here? Mostly the answers are those of theologians, philosophers, physicists and others who are thought to have some special pipeline to the eternal mysteries.

But all of us wonder why we are here. It is a question that occurs to little boys and girls playing with their toys; to college students; to plumbers, teachers, U.S. senators, nurses, soldiers, the homeless, ship captains and chief executive officers.

Their answers are rarely found in Bartlett's or any other compilation of quotations; yet the wisest men admit that the answer is beyond philosophy and science. So we might as well listen to Yogi Berra's answer as Emerson's or Einstein's.

In a recent issue, Life magazine asked a number of people, including sages, poets, scholars, athletes and tradesmen to answer the question. It published their answers under the title, "The Meaning of Life."

The answers ranged from the poetic and profound to the profane and scatological. Some agreed with Supreme Court Justice Harry Blackmun that "with our finite minds we cannot presume to know if there is a Purpose." Former boxer Muhammad Ali said that "life on earth is only a preparation for the eternal home." Businessman Armand Hammer said that we are here "to do good."

There was just as much truth, it seemed to me, in the more irreverent answer of a taxi driver, Jose Martinez, who said, "We're here to die; just to live and die.... Life is a big fake." Or a barber, Frank Domofrio, who said, "I've been asking why

I'm here most of my life. If there's a purpose, I don't care anymore. I'm 74. I'm on my way out." Or comedian Jackie Mason, who said, " 'What is the meaning of life?' is a stupid question. Life just exists...I see life as a dance. Does a dance have to have a meaning? You're dancing because you enjoy it."

Writer Charles Bukowski's answer was anti-Establishment: "We are here to unlearn the teachings of the church, state and our educational system. We are here to drink beer. We are here to kill war."

Many of the people quoted in Jon Winokur's book "Zen to Go" (New American Library) tease the question in the mysterious way of Zen. He catches former Gov. Jerry Brown saying, "Life just is. You have to flow with it. Give yourself to the moment. Let it happen." (No wonder columnist Mike Royko called him Moonbeam.) Writer Andre Gide says simply, "Life eludes logic," which is about all that Domofrio was saying. And philosopher Santayana says, "There is no cure for birth and death, save to enjoy the interval."

The late Richard P. Feynman, the Caltech physicist and Nobel Prize winner, turned the question upon itself:

I wonder why. I wonder why.

I wonder why I wonder.

I wonder why I wonder why.

I wonder why I wonder.

As far as we know, Feynman never found the answer.

Winokur quotes the beatnik novelist Jack Kerouac as saying, "I don't know. I don't care. And it doesn't make any difference."

In a similar mood, author Edward Abbey is quoted as saying, "What is truth? I don't know, and I'm sorry I brought it up."

And writer H. L. Mencken, with his usual blunt cynicism, said, "We are here, and it is now. Further than that, all human knowledge is moonshine."

Two sage observations on the danger of thought come from Yogi Berra, that uncut diamond of the baseball park, and O. J. Simpson, the great running back. Berra: "How can you think and hit at the same time?" And Simpson: "Thinking...is what gets you caught from behind."

The plain-spoken writer Gertrude Stein is given a special place at the front of the book: "There ain't no answer. There ain't going to be any answer. There never has been an answer. That's the answer."

But we keep searching. I remember grappling with the question one night when I was 18 as I lay on a boxcar near Riverside, looking at the stars. The closest I came then, and ever since, is that the purpose of life is to keep on living and see what happens next.

And we should be good to others and do what we can to end war.

Assuming the Role of Grouch Potato

Thursday, July 6, 1978

THE OTHER DAY I quoted here a letter from a woman who had written me to complain that she was old and lonely and isolated, living on a street of younger people in Hermosa Beach, and she needed some attention.

I am pleased that I have received many letters offering help and companionship, but there are also some suggestions that she may be self-indulgent.

"Your old lady is like many," writes James de Bree of Laguna Beach. "They become leaners early in life. They assume, then announce, that somebody owes them tender loving care all the rest of their days. And when they don't get it they begin wallowing in self-pity.

"True, she needs help, now. But we can be sure that she did little or nothing to prepare herself, either financially or emotionally, for her very old age...."

"Did any of the old and lonely," writes Del Reynolds of Balboa, "mention when they were 50 or 20 years younger, they went knocking on an older person's door? The friendly and considerate always have friends."

"I am an old lady," writes Helen Constable of Los Angeles. "I live alone, have no car and no relatives who are close by, but my experiences are totally different from your correspondent from Hermosa. A month ago I was mugged and received a hip injury. Since my return from the hospital I have not missed a single meal. My wonderful neighbors come on their way to work to prepare my breakfast, leave box lunches, and take orders for my market needs. They have arranged a schedule for dinners. One night the dinner is American, another Japanese, the next night the little lady from London brings the British roast beef."

It's possible, I suppose, that the woman in Hermosa Beach is rather disagreeable, and her neighbors simply can't put up with her. I have an idea that when I reach her age, if I am lucky enough to hold together that long, I will be crotchety, opinionated and boring, and will be methodically avoided by all my neighbors.

It is already beginning to happen. Just last week I was visited by a physicist, a poet and an architect, and if I'm not mistaken, each of them left with a determination never to come back. My lawyer is coming to see me this week, and I must try to be amiable, because I can't afford to lose her.

Actually, my physicist is a brilliant and intuitive man, but he is obsessed with the notion that time can be reversed, which of course is nonsense, and I have told him so. He is probably the

No. 1 scientist in the world on time reversal, and I am pleased that my skepticism amuses him.

The architect is a young neighbor of mine named Joseph Giovannini, and he has produced a book called "Los Angeles at 25 m.p.h.: Residences," to be published this fall by Ward Ritchie. The concept is excellent. Slow down, he says, and you can discover our city. Where else can you find, within one block, a Tudor mansion, a Mediterranean villa, a Taj Mahal, a French chateau?

I found his ideas most agreeable until he said that people would be happier living together in apartment houses than in the isolated yards that most of us live in here in our suburbs. I like my isolation. I don't want to hear my neighbor's plumbing, or get his mail. I have two acres, and in the morning, when I get up and look out my window, I feel baronial. "This is mine," I say. Tenements are overrated.

I think I also offended the poet, Georgia Alwan, who called on me with her delightful little daughter. She brought me this year's book of poems by pupils of Mt. Washington Elementary school. She and her husband have been helping children to express themselves through poetry, with splendid results.

She called my attention to a particular poem which, evidently, she thought was the best of the lot. I will quote only enough of it, I hope, to make my point.

I am on an antique ferris wheel...
It's a foggy day.
I look down on my wrist.
There is a birthmark...
I tremble with fright
Then I look at my other wrist.
Another birthmark!
"Hmm," I said. "Pretty depressing."
"You find it negative?"

"Yes," I said, feeling old and crotchety. I would say that when a poem is concerned with fog, birthmarks and fright, it is negative.

Ms. Alwan shook her head, and I had the feeling that she would not come back again.

Perhaps those who criticize the woman in Hermosa Beach are right. If you want company, you have to be agreeable.

I Can Name That Goon in One Word

Sunday, January 6, 1991

J AY H ELLER recommends to me a parlor game that he finds tougher and more revealing than inventing one's own epitaph.

"I call it 'Describe Yourself in One Word,' " he says. "My wife and I have played it at dinner parties a number of times with very interesting results."

I don't know why civilized people would need parlor games to entertain themselves when they have company. Perhaps we are so conditioned to watching television that we don't know what to do when we are a group and can't agree on what to watch.

More than one party has been ruined, I imagine, when the host insisted on watching a football or basketball game while his guests sat around in numb isolation. Few TV shows since "Roots" have been equally engaging for a diverse party of people.

Heller's game would force one to be introspective and self-revealing—not that that is invariably a good idea. More likely, each guest would try to think of a word that represented his best qualities, or summarized some fantasy he entertained about himself.

Heller says the word he chose for himself was *survivor,* since he has worked for advertising agencies for 50 years. His wife, Marian, has been a registered nurse for a similar time. She chose *nurturing.*

Some personalities are easily encapsulated. Charles Manson, if he were honest, would describe himself as a *psychopath.* Mother Teresa might call herself a *humanist.* Jim Bakker might call himself a *sinner.*

Of course, most of us, if we were completely honest, would describe ourselves as sinners. That might cause the party to degenerate into an embarrassment of questions and confessions.

If that game becomes tiresome, there's another that Heller suggests: "If You Had Your Choice of Anyone Living (or dead—the next version), Whom Would You Like to Have Dinner With Tomorrow Night?"

I'd like to have dinner with Margaret Thatcher. I'd like to ask her about her husband. When she was prime minister, did he cook? Did he put out the dog? Did he decide what TV shows they watched? Did he get to talk? Did he ever advise her to cool it? Is he a male chauvinist pig?

If I could have dinner with anyone who is dead, I'd like to have dinner with Cleopatra, provided we could surmount the language barrier. I have always thought of Cleo as a whirlwind of passions. I'm afraid, though, that I would bore her. She'd always be looking over my shoulder for some new Caesar.

"You can guess the next variation," Heller says. " 'Whom Would You Like to Sleep With Tomorrow Night?' "

I doubt that my group would care to play that game. One's sexual fantasies are best kept to oneself. It's too likely that one guest might confess that he'd like most to sleep with another's spouse. That sort of revelation can hardly be dismissed as amusing. But I have been avoiding the point. We started out with the game "Describe Yourself in One Word."

We are all too complex to be described in one word, but since that is the rule of the game, we must try. I think of several words that might define me to some degree: Kind. Generous. Thoughtful. Humane. Compassionate. Generous.

But essentially, I'm ignorant. I don't understand our times. I don't understand our culture. I don't understand our technology. I don't understand myself.

My word is *befuddled*.

Who's Afraid of the Big, Bad Everything?

Sunday, August 7, 1988

I HAVE a pet theory that we are all afraid of the wrong things. Fear is blind. It does not contain the faculty of foresight.

I have mentioned the woman in Honolulu who was worried about an earthquake a few days before Pearl Harbor. Thousands of Angelenos feared a big earthquake last May because of some irresponsible talk on TV about the alleged predictions of that notorious fraud and bad poet, Nostradamus.

Much has been said about the fear of combat.

I have often wondered what makes men go into combat. I believe that it is fear of being thought a coward by one's peers. I suppose some men are truly brave. It was not bravery that motivated me.

John Keegan, the British historian, reveals in "The Face of Battle," his excellent study of soldiers in battle, that in medieval times, and particularly at the battle of Agincourt, the men were drunk.

Alas, no such false courage was offered soldiers in World War II, though many officers had a bottle in their packs.

Even in World War I, the soldier's weapon was a machine, and drunkenness was not a help in its use. Today's technology calls for heroic sobriety.

Probably most of us still fear the phenomena we feared as children: the dark, being alone, monsters and ghosts, animals and insects, doctors and dentists, strangers, loud noises and so on.

A chart published recently in U.S. News & World Report (reprinted from Children magazine) reports that 59% of all children between the ages of 3 and 6 are afraid of the dark and that darkness leads every other cause of fear.

By the time we reach adulthood most of us have outgrown our fear of the dark.

It has become our friend. It shields us from our enemies. It promotes sleep. It shuts out the frantic day. It provides a benevolent cover for making love.

Fifty percent of children 3 to 6 years old fear being alone. Naturally, having been thrust into this world in complete ignorance of its ways, and needing almost constant attention, they *would* be afraid of being alone.

I am always seeking evidence of my adulthood. Perhaps I can find it in the fact that I no longer fear being alone, at least not for short periods of time.

I am quite content with my own company, unless my wife gets home from work too late. Then I begin to wonder who's going to cook my dinner.

I no longer fear monsters and ghosts, not even those produced by the wizards of special effects in movies. The only monsters I fear are human. Ghosts do not exist.

Most of our fears are of general calamities. We fear war

because we know it is a possibility. We fear earthquakes because we know they are probable. We fear death because we know it is certain.

Most of us, though, foresee death in the wrong guise.

We fear we will be shot by gangs, when we are more likely to die in bed. We fear we will die in an airplane crash, when we are more likely to die of drink.

I myself am afraid that I will die of old age, which I probably will.

What else am I afraid of, now that most of the common childhood fears are behind me?

Well, eliminate the dark, ghosts and monsters and being alone, and I'm still afraid of most all the things children are afraid of.

I'm afraid of loud noises, heights, going fast and natural disasters.

I'm not exactly *afraid* of doctors and dentists, but for some reason my blood pressure rises whenever I visit one.

Most of all, like everyone else, I am afraid of making a social *faux pas*.

We are cowards all.

Last Flight of the Bungled Bee

Monday, May 15, 1989

"I HEAR A BEE," my wife said the other day when we were both in the kitchen.

I heard it too. She handed me the fly swatter. I am deadly with a fly swatter. The stroke is swift and true. It is one of the few athletic skills I have left.

"There it is," she said, "in the window."

It was against the window pane above the sink. I raised the swatter to deliver a fatal swat. Then I realized that the bee was trapped in an invisible web. Its wings were moving but it obviously couldn't fly. Now and then it would throw its whole body into a frenzied effort to escape. It was like a seizure. Then, evidently exhausted, it would simply hang there, as if appraising its situation.

Then I saw the spider. It was suspended, also in an invisible web, about three inches above the trapped bee. I lowered the swatter. "Might as well let nature take its course," my wife said, reading my mind.

I was tempted to interfere, but I wasn't sure I could. If I killed the spider, the bee would still be entangled. If I tried to free the bee, it would probably sting me. Besides, I probably couldn't free it from the web without breaking its wings.

Anyway, I thought, what right did I have to interfere in this dance of death? It happened every second of every day. The hunter and the prey. I remembered Tennyson's line:

Nature, red in tooth and claw

It was God's doing. From the protozoa on up, one species preyed upon another. Who was I to intrude?

Of course we killed foxes and weasels to protect our chickens, but that was different. In that case the predators had intruded on our establishment, threatening our own prey. That man would protect his chickens was a part of the divine equation.

One does not like to kill bees. They make honey. They are industrious. They have qualities that we admire. On the other hand, spiders are sinister. They are venomous, although only a very few are dangerous to man. But they are cruel and relentless hunters. We are even told that in some species the females eat their mates after copulation. That habit has been translated into a human metaphor as the "spider woman."

I used to kill spiders on sight. But somewhere along the line I learned that they were beneficial. A spider in the house kept even more unlovely creatures from proliferating. Some house spiders are even thought of as good omens, like lizards in Hawaii.

Years ago I killed a tarantula that was crawling up our screen door; but I regretted it. I could have spared it. Since then I have never killed a spider, except black widows when they turned up in the garage. I regard black widows as one of God's mistakes. I have even rescued spiders from my bathtub and transferred them outdoors, where they undoubtedly fell prey to one of their other enemies.

We watched. The spider began making swift runs down its web to the bee. It touched the bee with its legs. The bee reacted violently, turning itself upside down in the web in its terror. The spider quickly withdrew. From a distance of two inches it kept an eye on its prey. Then, every minute or so, it would go down to the bee like a trapeze artist going down a ladder. Each time it would reach out toward the bee and the bee would go into one of its terrible exertions. And again the spider would withdraw. Once or twice, it seemed to me, the spider got close enough to bite the bee with its fearful pincers. Every spider, I have read, is equipped with fangs that secrete poison.

The spider was exquisitely careful, but unrelenting. Again and again it touched the bee with its kiss of death. Finally I tired of the prolonged ritual and went into the living room to finish my coffee.

Maybe 15 minutes later I went back to the window. The spider had drawn the bee to the upper corner of the window, and now had it in its fatal embrace. The bee was still, its struggle ended. It was merely a carcass. The spider, as we knew it would, had won.

Que sera, sera.

If the 'Big One' Doesn't Get You, the Pyramid Will

Sunday, January 28, 1990

IT'S A LITTLE LATE in the new year to be bringing this up, but something called the National Anxiety Center in Maplewood, N.J., has published a list of the Top 10 things to worry about in 1990.

The list also includes 90 other things to worry about, but we probably shouldn't worry about them, because the center's point is that we ought to set some priorities, so we don't worry about everything.

As a person who tends to be a worrier, I really don't need the list. I have my own priorities.

I worry mostly about things that aren't going to happen. As my wife says, on vacation trips I always carry a bag of worst scenarios.

Just to get them out of the way, here are the anxiety center's Top 10: AIDS, drug abuse, nuclear waste, the ozone layer, famine, the homeless, the federal deficit, air pollution, water pollution and garbage.

Those are formidable bugaboos indeed. They give us a sense of despair. They seem to be rushing toward us like a tidal wave.

I have no idea how to alleviate any of them. Alan Caruba, executive director of the NAC, hasn't either.

"People ask the center if we have any solutions to these problems," he says. "Frankly, we haven't the slightest clue."

Maybe the anxiety center has taken its cue from the Transcendental Meditation folks, who believe that if enough people meditate about the stock market or China or the Israeli-Palestinian problem, they can alter such matters in a favorable fashion.

If everyone in the country were to worry simultaneously about the ozone layer, could that protect it? Perhaps—if their worry prodded them into doing what has to be done.

The trouble is, most of us worry only about the calamities that may overtake us as individuals. I worry about an earthquake.

I suppose that the Big One will level the city, but all I can think about is my own house.

I worry that the earthquake will not only destroy our house but will destroy it just as our remodeling is about to be finished, thus leaving us not only homeless but in financial ruin as well.

I worry that when the Big One comes, I will either be riding in an elevator or driving through the 2nd Street tunnel. If I became trapped in an elevator with several other victims, my claustrophobia would kill me. Being buried alive in the tunnel would be worse than death.

Though the NAC doesn't mention it, I worry that a comet will strike the Earth, killing me. That's quite possible. Some scientists believe that a comet wiped out the dinosaurs 60 million years ago. There's no reason to believe that one couldn't get me.

I worry that when my wife and I go to Egypt (if we do), the Great Pyramid will collapse and bury me in it. The fact that it has stood firm for 4,500 years is no reason to believe that it won't collapse while I'm in it. If things are going to happen, they're going to happen.

I worry that I will buy myself a winning lottery ticket but that I will forget to find out the winning numbers and will go on never knowing that I have won.

What I don't know won't hurt me, of course, but that doesn't keep me from worrying about it.

I worry that our income tax returns will be audited—and we will have nothing to hide. One of our tax men said my wife and I were the most honest taxpayers in his experience. That doesn't mean the auditors couldn't find something. Even with expert help, nobody can file a tax return that something can't be found wrong with.

Sometimes I worry that I will be caught in a traffic jam on the Santa Ana Freeway and will die.

I do not worry about a heart attack, since my bypass is supposed to protect me from that, but I worry that in a traffic jam on the Santa Ana Freeway I will die of old age. I worry that I will die either of having too much cholesterol or not enough. One day I read that cholesterol is good for you, and the next that it will kill you. I've decided to leave it alone.

I worry that I will die of malathion poisoning. We live in one of the areas that they sprayed by helicopter. I can't believe that anything that will kill fruit flies is good for me.

One of the anxiety center's Top 10 things was garbage. Garbage used to be kitchen scraps, and everything else was trash. I worry that the distinction has been lost.

Washing Dishes vs. Population Explosion

Monday, October 10, 1994

IN WONDERING the other day about why we are here (a subject plainly beyond my philosophical reach), I suggested that if God is infallible—as many of us believe—why did he do such a bad job of it when he created humankind?

Why, I asked, did he create two sexes, and leave the procreation of the species to sexual union, an arrangement that causes all kinds of trouble. I have received several letters scoffing at this question, some suggesting that I myself must have enjoyed that arrangement.

"You dangerously strolled into Abby's and Ann's domain this morning," writes Michele Yepiz.

"Sexual union is, to my mind," writes Frank Wentink, "although I have been unable to indulge for some years because of the infirmities of old age, still remembered as the most glorious of all sensations when indulged in by two persons who love each other.

"Obviously," he concedes, "even people who don't love each other must find it so, judging from the large number of illegitimate children being born in these times. After reading your column for many years it is difficult for me to imagine you never enjoyed sex."

Perish the thought. That is the trouble with sweeping philosophical statements.

Yet that is exactly my point. If sex were not so enjoyable, it would not be so widely practiced, and the world would not be moving toward a dreadful population explosion.

The Earth's population today is increasing at the rate of three persons per second, or about a quarter of a million every day. That will be an increase of one billion by the year 2000. Where are we going to put us?

Supposing God had arranged that men and women did not produce children by having sex, but by washing the dishes together? Surely that would cut down considerably on the birth rate.

Of course, we didn't have dishes until the species was several thousand years old, but surely God could have found some other, less enjoyable way to procreate.

Let me leave the question of why we are here for a moment to consider three other questions of cosmic consequence reported by the press in the past week.

First, astronomers have discovered that the universe is only about half as old as many of the oldest stars and galaxies it contains. That is a paradox. We have always thought the universe included everything. Every last particle. How can it be younger than some of its parts?

I'll leave that one to the astronomers.

The second startling news story was about the discovery of the missing link. For decades, scientists have been searching for the bones of a creature that links human beings and the apes.

Now they think they have found it in Ethiopia. It is only a handful of teeth and skull fragments, but they are about a million years older than any other bones found in the human family tree.

"This species," says Tim D. White, a paleontologist, "is the oldest known link in the evolutionary chain that connected us to the common ancestor (we share) with the living African apes."

Creationists who doubt Darwinian theory have always thrown "the missing link" at scientists who insist evolution is not theory, but fact. "Where's the missing link?" they'd say. Now, evidently, we have it.

The third news story, in the New York Times, is rather more disturbing.

About a billion years from now, it says, the sun's increasing brightness may evaporate Earth's water.

Then, on its way to becoming a red star, the sun will burn its various gases, with periodic explosions. Finally, some 12.4 billion years after its birth, it will undergo the last of its spasmodic helium explosions. The dying sun will form "a planetary nebula, a small hot stellar remnant."

"Further cooling will leave the sun as a white dwarf," the article says, "consisting of matter so dense that one cubic inch would weigh about 10 tons. At the end of the trail the sun will become a black dwarf orbited by the cinders of its former planetary system, including the frozen remnant of the long lifeless Earth. There Earth will continue to spin, perhaps forever."

I was discussing these matters at lunch with Herb Henrikson, a Caltech scientist, and asked him what he thought about the inevitable end.

He said he was reminded of the story about the little old lady who was informed that all these dreadful things would happen in 12 billion years.

"Oh dear!" she exclaimed. "In only 12 million years!"

"Twelve *billion* years, not million," she was informed.

"Thank God!" she said.

As one of the scientists quoted by the New York Times said: "Fortunately we still have lots and lots of time."

To do what?

Celebrating Seder With Their Extended Family

Wednesday, April 3, 1985

W E W E N T to a Seder the other night.

I had never been to a Seder. I am not a Jew. I am not a religious person.

But Rabbi Alfred Wolf, of the Wilshire Boulevard Temple, was holding this Seder in the interests of brotherhood, and he knows I believe in that.

He had invited the congregation of the Second Baptist Church, a landmark of the black community, to share the feast in the temple with his own congregation.

Seder is usually celebrated on the evening of the first day of Passover. This one was several days before that. "By magic," Rabbi Wolf explained, "the calendar has just been changed." He sat at a head table beside the Rev. Thomas Kilgore Jr. of the Second Baptist Church, along with their associates in the two churches, and their wives.

Passover, of course, is the eight-day Jewish celebration of the escape of the ancient Hebrews from slavery in Egypt, as described in Exodus. It generally coincides with Easter week.

"Seder," the rabbi said, "is the experience of a Jewish family. Tonight we are all one family. We are brothers, sisters, parents, cousins, aunts, nieces. Pastor Kilgore and I are the fathers of the family. We have all had the experiences of slavery and freedom at some stage of our lives."

At each setting, fortunately, we found a Haggadah—a book explaining the ritual and containing the words to be spoken and songs to be sung. The table, it said, should have a candelabra and a festive tablecloth. There should be three pieces of matzo; a roasted lamb shank bone, representing the lamb sacrifice made on the eve of the Exodus; bitter herbs (a slice of horseradish), representing the bitterness of slavery; a sprig of parsley, for spring, and a small dish of saltwater to dip it in; *charoset*, a mixture of grated apples, chopped walnuts, honey and wine, symbolizing the mortar from which the Jews were forced to make bricks for the Pharaoh; a roasted egg, whose significance, I learned, is debated.

All these things we found. Plus a goblet of wine at each setting and a pitcher of wine.

Not knowing whether that forbidding fare was to be our entire meal or not, I was thankful at least for the wine.

"We will have to work a little magic on the wine, too," the rabbi said. "It is unfermented, so that it may be enjoyed by all ages."

I doubted that magic would work. It would take a miracle.

The rabbi then began the reading from the Haggadah:

"With family and friends we gather now to celebrate the festival of Pesach. With song and rejoicing we will commemorate our people's exodus from Egypt, and our ancient yearning for the liberation of all humanity from bondage...."

Variously, the rabbi, the minister and members of the two congregations read from the book as the ceremony proceeded.

As at each table the candles were lighted, someone read:

May the festival lights we now kindle
Inspire us to use our human powers....
To serve the God of freedom.

How natural it seemed for these two peoples to be celebrating freedom together; both had suffered the curse of slavery throughout their history, and neither was yet fully free.

In time we dipped the parsley in saltwater and ate it.

For behold the winter is past,

The rains are over and gone.
The blossoms have appeared in the land.
The time of singing is here.

We sipped our grape juice, then everyone joined in the singing of the Hebrew prayer: *Baruch Atah Adonai Eloheinu Melech ha-olam borei p'ri ha-gafen.* (Be praised, Eternal our God, Ruler of the universe, Who creates the fruit of the vine.)

I wondered in what dreadful circumstances the Seder had been celebrated at other times in Jewish history; how had they managed, in their faith, to keep the tradition alive in the concentration camps. Was there even then some bitter herb? Unleavened bread?

We celebrated this night in a bright room on the third floor of the temple, with six glittering chandeliers hanging from the vaulted ceiling over the main chamber and smaller ones over the alcoves along each side. Slender Ionic columns separated the two. It was a long way from the wilderness.

There was, after all, a complete dinner, succulent roast chicken and vegetables and cake; and wine, if one could make the magic work.

Everyone joined in the singing of the hymn:
When Israel was in Egypt land
Let my people go.
Oppressed so hard they could not stand.
Let my people go.
Go down Moses
Way down in Egypt's land;
Tell old Pharaoh,
Let my people go.

So an ancient Hebrew lament had found voice in the spiritual music of America's blacks.

I do not sing in public. But toward the end, when everyone stood to hold hands and sing "We Shall Overcome," I found myself holding my wife's hand on one side and the hand of a young black man on the other, and I was singing:

We shall overcome, We shall overcome
We shall overcome some day.
Oh, deep in my heart I do believe
We shall overcome some day....

Finally, we sang "My Country, 'Tis of Thee," and I sang that, too.

From every mountainside,
Let freedom ring.

In closing, Rabbi Wolf said: "We do not want to engage in empty symbolism. We want to start a process, which, if we do it right, will bring people together."

I believe in that, too.

CHAPTER 9

The Labors of My Love

Conserving Her Energy
for His Well-Being

Thursday, June 22, 1989

IN ONE of my rare scientific studies a couple of years ago I tried to explain the word *entropy*, which can't be done short of a turgid doctorate.

According to Webster's, the meaning closest to the one I have in mind is "a measure of the degree of disorder in a substance or a system: entropy always increases and available energy diminishes in a closed system, as the universe."

Entropy is also used to describe the second law of thermodynamics, which is that "every time energy is transformed from one state to another 'a certain penalty is exacted.' That penalty is a loss in the amount of available energy to perform work of some kind in the future."

But we don't have to understand that. All we have to understand is that everything is running down and sooner or later everything will come to a stop. That is entropy on the grand scale.

On the smaller scale, it is happening to our house. We have lived in the same house 39 years and the inroads of entropy are obvious. For one thing the major source of energy, me, is slowing down. My wife is still going like a dynamo, but she can't do it all by herself.

There are small telltale events. For months the hanging lamp over my wife's bed was out. New light bulbs did not work. It was in the wiring. One day I took it down and removed the part you screw the bulb into. I have been carrying it around in my car ever since.

Meanwhile, my wife took down the lamp from the adjoining twin bed and hung it over hers. Temporarily, she has light, but the other bed is in darkness.

The wooden steps to our service porch have long since rotted out. One day a young plumber put the *coup de grace* to them when he was climbing them with a new water heater (the old one had blown out) and he crashed through them. Happily, he was not hurt.

Two large slabs of the swimming pool deck had been sinking on one side and tilting up on the other. The cracks were unsightly and dangerous. With some of my remaining energy, I recently hired a man to replace them, at a cost of $550.

At the same time he used concrete to replace the steps down from the dog yard, which had been made of redwood ties and brick, and were crumbling. That was $200. It taught me that one way to reverse entropy is to pay someone to combat it. While it lasts, energy can be hired.

But something other than energy is a factor here. It is will. One must bestir oneself to get something done, if it is only to hire help. I have yet to do anything serious about the roof leak. Ever since we had the bedroom wing widened by six feet, the roof over the bedrooms has leaked. I know it must be fixed, but we keep putting it off because my wife wants to add a second floor, and that would obviate it.

I have written before about the clutter. That is a different thing from entropy. Trying to set an example for my wife, I have recently taken several hundred books from my shelves and piled them up about the house to give to some needy library. I have yet to offer them; they remain in unstable piles by the front door, in the den, in the living room. In the sense that I haven't taken any final action, they are products of entropy.

Entropy is compounded by regression. My wife wants to add a laundry to our kitchen. For years we have been taking our wash out to a Laundromat; now she wants to wash at home again. I regard this not only as a betrayal of the feminist code but a waste of money. Besides, I think we ought to conserve whatever energy she has left. If entropy is going to get us, it's certainly going to get me first.

Obviously we have come to a critical conflict. As entropy closes in, I want to lighten ship: condense, eliminate. She wants to expand, to widen our horizons, to create new arenas for the expenditure of our dwindling energies.

She wants to defy entropy, and she will.

Her Work and No Play Makes Jack a Tired Boy

Tuesday, July 25, 1989

THAT OLD REFRAIN "Thank God it's Friday" has become meaningless as urban life becomes ever more demanding and stressful and we keep putting chores off until the weekend.

Few of us have the time on weekends any more to escape to the golf course, or go on picnics, or just lie about the house catching up on the paper or dozing in front of the television set.

Even at our age, without children underfoot, we are so busy on weekends doing chores that we are glad to see Monday roll around and restore us to a normal schedule.

Hilton Hotels, its interest being obvious, recently commissioned a study of the deteriorating weekend and found that 90% of Americans feel no more energetic at the end of the weekend than they do on Friday.

"Americans spend almost half their weekend time (14

hours) doing chores," the study concluded, "such as cleaning, laundry, grocery shopping, errands, household repairs, paying bills and working at their jobs.

"Despite major strides in equality, women still work over an hour more than men during the weekend; 2½ hours more if you include time spent cooking."

Kids, of course, make it tougher. "People with children spend 66% more weekend time cleaning, 43% more time cooking and 52% more time doing laundry than those without children."

Whatever happened to afternoons in the park, fishing trips to mountain streams, days at the beach, drives in the country—all those diversions that used to set the weekend apart from the work week?

Life magazine recently had a spread about a young working mother's 133-hour work week. It was a horror story. It concluded that working mothers put in from 13 to 15 more hours a week than their husbands (because they have to take care of *them* as well as their children).

My wife is up every morning at 6:30. She makes coffee, feeds the dogs and cats, brings in the paper and makes her breakfast. I get up around 8 and make my own breakfast, so that's one thing she doesn't have to do.

By 9 my wife is off to the office. I read the paper and then go to work in my den. I do some writing and much reading of correspondence. I try to answer some letters, but I am always far behind. At 1:30 I make some lunch. I finish reading the paper and take a nap. In the late afternoon I go back to work.

My wife rarely gets home before 7. She has to prepare dinner by 8 or 8:30, usually microwave. There's no time for cooking. While we eat we watch a movie on TV. After the movie she works on our accounts, usually until midnight. I no longer have time to read books until after I've gone to bed.

On Saturday mornings my wife gathers up the laundry and drives it to the Laundromat, picking up our previous week's laundry. She stops at the supermarket to shop for the week. She usually spends the rest of the day doing other shopping chores.

In the late afternoon she works in the yard until dark. Then she cooks dinner and we watch television while she irons. Before going to bed she does some more paper work. It is never finished.

Sometimes on Sunday mornings she cooks bacon and eggs for both of us, after feeding the dogs and cats and bringing in the paper. Then, while I read the paper, she washes her intimate clothing and things she doesn't trust to the laundry. Sometimes she washes a shirt or two of mine, though I don't like her to.

After reading the paper I go to work writing or answering letters. After lunch my wife goes out to some plant sale or works in the yard. Sometimes I spend a part of the afternoon watching some sports event on TV or taking a nap. That is my recreation. She works in the yard. She microwaves dinner before 9, and we watch television while she irons.

Of course Hilton suggests that you hole up in one of their hotels for the weekend. Get away from it all. But who'd do the ironing? Who'd pay the bills? Who'd do the yardwork?

It's just possible that I might get away for a weekend; but my wife couldn't be spared.

An Out-of-Focus Plan
for Her Rogue's Gallery

Sunday, September 23, 1990

I HAVE BEEN TRYING to think of what we can throw away to lighten our impedimenta when our remodeling is finished and we move into our new quarters.

You might think that with more space we would have no need to lighten ship. But I see it as a way of getting rid of all the junk we have acquired over 40 years. I have already suggested several perfectly obvious kinds of things that never would be missed: first, my wife's 1,000 cookbooks; second, her hundreds of old magazines; third, many of her clothes. She will not budge. We don't even talk about it anymore.

On my part, I have already given away several hundred of my books and plan to give away more. I have given away several suits and shirts. I also had decided to throw out a few thousand of my columns that my wife pasted up in notebooks, but she has already rescued them and photocopied every one.

I was in my wife's room watching TV today, and, during a commercial, my eye happened to fall on the gallery of family photographs on her wall. Why is it that women insist on displaying photographs of their relatives?

Nothing would be less likely to be missed, it occurred to me, than that gallery.

I studied them individually. When photographs have been up on a wall for years, one never notices them. I looked at some of them as if for the first time. Their range, in time, was incredible.

Of course, nothing can be done about the obligatory

photographs of our grandchildren. They are shown at various ages and in various combinations. I suppose some place will have to be found for them.

But why do we have a picture of me and my wife, obviously a posed portrait taken by a professional photographer, when I was in my Marine uniform? Oh, I agree, we were quite handsome, but why must one be reminded of that?

There is also a portrait of my wife's father and mother in their wedding clothes. I suppose it is precious to my wife, and I could hardly ask her to toss it.

For that matter, I am rather fond of a snapshot of my mother and father, taken in the 1920s in front of our house. He is wearing a sporty suit and a Panama hat. I imagine his Chrysler roadster was parked nearby.

There is also a framed snapshot of my wife and me in Copenhagen on our way back from Russia. I am amazed at how good I looked in that Russian hat. I believe it was a worker's hat.

Some of them are silly. There is one of me, for example, taken when I was living in Hawaii. I am standing in my swimming trunks beside a palm tree. My hair is tousled from a swim. I have a hibiscus over one ear and am holding another in my teeth. My hands are clenched behind me to emphasize the musculature of my chest (which wasn't much). Well, nothing would be lost if that picture vanished, but I suppose it means something to my wife.

A rare picture from my own family album shows me standing on a bench beside my mother. She was quite beautiful, and she wears an elegant gown of lace. For a 2-year-old, I look extraordinarily intelligent. That picture, too, was obviously posed for a professional photographer. The only thing I can remember about the circumstances is that my shoes belonged to my cousin Betty Mae; mine were too scuffed.

There is a tiny snapshot in an oval frame of a small boy and girl walking off down a sidewalk with their backs to the camera. The girl wears a white dress and a pinafore; the boy wears a sailor suit. The girl has long curls and a large bow. They are holding hands: my brother and sister walking off to school.

There is a picture of my wife in jodhpurs, leaning against a fence. That reminded me that we once owned a horse that was blind in one eye and had only one gait—a full-out run. But at least my wife was properly attired.

A large, framed picture shows our sons sitting on the back steps. Their clothing is in tatters. They look like children of the Depression. Our younger son is wearing shorts and a ripped white T-shirt. I remember he was attired like that one Sunday when my wife drove to The Times and sent him up to the newsroom to get some money from me. When he left, my colleagues took up a collection to buy him some clothes.

There are pictures of our two sons' wedding parties, framed in gold.

Oh, well, throwing them out was probably not a very good idea.

No Micro Brings On Waves
of Nostalgia

Wednesday, August 22, 1990

"BUT THIS IS 1990," Beverly Beyette wrote recently in this section, "and, popular wisdom has it, family dinner time is all but extinct. Blame it on the women's movement, or Little League, or pizza-at-your-door...."

To the contrary, the body of her story pointed out, of 500

families with children studied in a Times survey, 86% said the family dinner hour was "very important," a finding borne out by a current UCLA study.

Of course my own household would not qualify for this study, since our children have long since gone, leaving us alone. I don't know whether a dinner for two persons can be called a family dinner, but even if it could be, I doubt that ours would qualify.

I don't blame the women's movement, Little League or pizza-at-your-door for the decline of our dinner hour. True, my wife is in the work force, and comes home late, but she always has time to pop a microwave dinner into the oven; Little League is no longer a factor, and I have never ordered a home-delivered pizza in my life.

In our house the culprit is television. For years now we have been eating at television trays. Each of us has an easy chair pointed at the TV set, and the trays are in front of the chairs. When my wife comes home she asks me what kind of microwave dinner I want and gives me two or three choices. While the dinner is in the oven I check the TV log to see if there is a movie we can watch. I check the movies out in Leonard Maltin's TV Movies and Video Guide. Its thumbnail reviews are usually very reliable.

Of course the movies last two hours, and the only time one has for conversation is during the commercial breaks. Usually, though, we just stare at the commercials, mesmerized.

We never eat at the dining room table anymore. It is hopelessly covered with correspondence, bills, magazines, catalogues and indescribable junk. Once a year, at Easter, it is cleaned off for a family dinner.

Recently we moved the table out of the dining room into the living room, to make way for the remodeling. We did not, however, clear it of its debris.

Then the other evening our French daughter-in-law called to say that she had a large batch of leftover lasagna and wondered if she made a salad and brought the two over, with her husband, we would like to have dinner with them.

"You mean *here*?" my wife said, not used to having guests to dinner. But of course she agreed. My daughter-in-law's lasagna is famous.

My wife cleaned off the table and when our guests arrived my son helped her carry it back into the dining room. The workers had already removed the overhead light.

"I guess we can use candles," my wife said, necessity forcing her return to an old custom.

"Why not?" my son said.

She got out the candles and lighted them and my daughter-in-law heated up the lasagna and I opened a bottle of red wine—that being my function. It was an idyllic, old-fashioned, stay-at-home dinner. At one point I said, "Shouldn't we have some music?" The idea was met with general enthusiasm.

I looked through my pile of compact discs, realizing I hadn't played one in months. Just because it was on top I selected the music from "Gone With the Wind." It was showy and colorful and nostalgic. For some reason we couldn't remember the name of Scarlett O'Hara, though Vivien Leigh gave us no trouble. Finally it came off the tip of my tongue, and everyone was much relieved.

The conversation sailed along at that level. My wife and I couldn't remember where we had first seen the movie, though she thought it must have been the Fox theater in Bakersfield. Recalling our Bakersfield years gave the talk a romantic turn.

I remembered poignantly the years when our two boys were still small and we had dinner together every evening— that is, when I was home. Sometimes I had to work late and sometimes I was late at the Press Club. But I remembered that when the boys sat at the table their feet didn't touch the floor. That always dramatized for me how small they were, and how dependent on us.

The lasagna was excellent. The wine was dry and of good vintage. In the candlelight we all looked human and civilized. If it was not brilliant, the conversation at least was not vulgar. The music reminded us that life is a bonbon.

We're thinking of trying it again some time.

Four Birds in a Cage
Are Worth One in a Tub

Sunday, January 13, 1991

M Y   W I F E ' S cockatiel died the other day. I don't know how old he was, but he seems to have been around almost as long as I have. I don't know what sex it was, but I always thought of it as a he, possibly because he was aggressive, mean-spirited and shrewish.

If anyone thinks that only females can be shrewish, I suggest that person is being sexist. Males make the worst shrews.

I had almost no contact with the bird. He stayed in his cage, I stayed in mine. But I was reminded of his presence every day. Evidently he disliked the world and kept it cognizant of that hostility by belaboring it throughout the day with shrill imprecations. His shriek, repeated intermittently, could rip my peace of mind to shreds.

A cockatiel is a kind of parrot. I believe it is South American in origin, which might account for this one's unhappiness here, away from his native rain forest. However, for a cockatiel, he may have been happy. His cage was in my wife's bathroom, which, because of her daily showers, was usually humid. He was rather an attractive bird, except for his hideous prehensile beak and predatory eyes. He was mostly white, with streaks of black and yellow about the head and shoulders. He had a topknot.

I don't believe he ever had a name. My wife called him Big Bird. She also has three parakeets and a canary. If any of them have names, she has never told me. I have no idea why she has birds. Nothing in her childhood predisposed her to keep birds. When I married her, I was unaware of this strange predilection.

Being members of the parrot family, cockatiels are supposed to be able to talk. The only conversation I ever had with Big Bird was when my wife went to France, leaving him in my care. Somehow, when I was trying to feed him, the bird got out. My wife has a three-foot-deep tiled bathtub. It takes athletic skill to get out of it. The bird made immediately for the tub and settled on the bottom, shrieking.

He ignored my entreaties to come out. Finally, I got down in the tub, grabbed the bird in one hand and tried to lift myself out of the tub with the other. Meanwhile, the bird sank his beak into the hand that held him. He was serious. His beak fastened onto my flesh and clamped down until I bled. The pain was excruciating.

Yelling obscenities at the bird at the top of my lungs, I climbed out of the tub, took two strides to his cage, shoved my hand in, wrenched it free from the bird's grasp with my free hand and slammed his door.

He glowered at me, heaving. "Big deal!" he said, quite clearly.

As far as I know, those are the only words he ever spoke.

"My Big Bird died yesterday," my wife told me simply.

She did not say how she'd disposed of the body, and I didn't ask.

The next day she said, "I miss my bird."

I pointed out that the bird had never tried to repay her for her love and care. He had rewarded her with nothing but looks of hatred from those glaring eyes, shrill protests and a recalcitrant rattling of his cage.

"He was company," she said. "I knew he was there."

I decided not to explore the implications of that remark.

The three parakeets are relatively quiet. They hop about in their common cage, chirping like old gossips. They seem to be happy, though how they can stand the confinement, I don't know.

The canary has a cage of his own. When my wife picked him out at Hal's Pet Shop, he was singing like Caruso. In recent months, however, he has fallen silent. Maybe he found out Caruso has been dead since 1921. He merely sits on a rung in his cage, fattening, and observing the limited world around him through his stupid little eyes.

Meanwhile, a reader writes that a friend has two parakeets that he bought at a pet store. "He is considering giving them freedom only if their chance of survival is good. If so, is spring the best time to let them go?"

I suspect that this correspondent's "friend" is himself. He doesn't want to admit that he is thinking of turning his parakeets out into the cold world. In any case, I am told that parakeets cannot survive in a natural environment. They would be easy marks for predators. My advice to this man, or his friend, is to free the birds on Mt. Washington. If history repeats itself, they will find their way to our door, and my wife will take them in.

Meanwhile, if anyone has any ideas about where to find homes for five wild cats, let me know.

Her Self-Esteem Is
His Household Task

Sunday, April 5, 1987

NOW THAT the women's movement is winding down in heat and intensity, I have an idea that many married or cohabiting couples have slipped back into their old sexist ways.

I sometimes wonder how many married women who hold jobs outside the home still do all the cooking and housekeeping. I have an idea it would be about 66%.

Of course, as a result of the movement, many sorts of accommodations have been worked out toward equality, as they have in our house.

Perhaps you have seen "L.A. Law," the TV series about a Los Angeles law firm and its loves, liaisons and, incidentally, lawsuits. In an early sequence we saw a man and a woman member of the firm leave a cocktail party and go to his place to make love. Considering that she is a tall, slender knockout and he is short and plump, though cute enough, to my mind their affair lacked plausibility.

Then I read in People magazine that this unlikely pair are actually married, in real life. She is 5-foot, 8-inch Jill Eikenberry; he is 5-foot, 5-inch Michael Tucker. What is pertinent here is a note on their "equal" living arrangements.

"We tend to slip back and forth into traditional roles," the magazine quotes Eikenberry as saying, "even though I consider myself a feminist."

Interjects Tucker: "So do I!"

Tucker does most of the cooking in the marriage, the magazine says, while Eikenberry leaves the dishes for the maid.

Now I consider that an absolutely ideal sharing of the burden. The husband does the cooking; the wife leaves the dishes for the maid.

What could be more equitable?

I read it to my wife.

She said, "So what?"

I said: "Why couldn't we do that? You do the cooking and I leave the dishes for the maid."

"You forget," she said, "I'm the maid."

We do have a cleaning woman, but she comes in only once a week, on Saturday morning, and changes the bed linen, mops the kitchen and bathroom floors, and vacuums the carpets.

That leaves a lot of work undone, which my wife and I try to share. Despite the concessions that we have made to liberation, there are a few things she still does by herself because she does them so much better than I do, and there would be no point in denying us both the quality of her work just to lighten her load.

I usually get my own breakfast and my own lunch, or I eat out; but she usually gets dinner after she comes home from work, which is not before 6:30 or 7 o'clock because of the freeway traffic.

That may seem unfair. But put yourself in her position. She either eats my cooking or she does the cooking herself.

Since we don't have a maid, she washes the dishes. When we were first married she wanted a dishwasher, but it was years before she got one. Now that she has one, I think it would be a shame to deny her the luxury of using it.

One thing I do, I put my breakfast and luncheon dishes in the washer to save her that trouble, but I don't actually operate it. I think that if you develop skill in the other person's field, it makes her feel less unique and useful. It's threatening. One of the main responsibilities of a spouse is to reinforce the other person's self-esteem.

For example, she washes my dress shirts. I complain constantly that I don't want her doing that, that she ought to send them out with the rest of the laundry. But she takes pride in turning out a well-finished shirt. How can I fight that?

You may wonder how she has prospered from liberation. For one thing, she used to make all three meals, and wash my underwear and socks and my dress shirts as well.

I used to give her money to run the house. Now she has all the money, which means, of course, that she gets to keep the books. All I do is ask her for some cash now and then, mostly to buy breakfast and lunch with, so she won't have to wash my dishes.

She also feeds the dogs and cats, but that's only fair, since they are all strays and she took them in. Of course I have nothing to do with her birds.

Meanwhile, I'm responsible for keeping my shoes and socks off the living room floor and for keeping the magazines in neat stacks. That's no easy job. We must get 30 magazines a month.

What I'm trying to say is that the feminist revolution hasn't entirely missed us, and I'm still trying to raise my consciousness even more.

But she resists it. I offer to cook. The freezer is stuffed with frozen dinners that I could easily pop into the microwave. She insists on doing it herself.

Recently I thought I had made some progress. I got her to send my dress shirts to the laundry. The collars came back terribly wrinkled.

"That's the last time I ever do that," she said.

Maybe we should get a maid. A maid wouldn't be threatening; and I could leave the dishes for her.

It would give me one more thing to do.

Bulbs Are Something
He Doesn't Take Lightly

Monday, September 8, 1986

M Y   W I F E found an item in one of her mail order catalogues that she thought might interest me.

She said, "It's a light bulb that lasts 60,000 hours, so you
never have to replace it."

I felt a twinge of anxiety.

"Sixty thousand hours?" I said.

"Yes, it says that's long enough to last 20 years, if you only
burn them eight hours a day."

"The way we leave lights on," I said evasively, "that would
only last us about 10 years."

Even so, I was worried. "Let me see it," I said.

The ad read: "You never have to change these bulbs. Standing on a ladder, or balancing on a chair, while trying to replace
a hard-to-reach light bulb in the dark, is one of our least
favorite chores. So we've replaced all our ordinary bulbs with
these patented Diolight Forever bulbs, guaranteed for 60,000
hours. That's 20 years, even at eight hours every day!"

I felt like an NFL quarterback whose contract has not been
renewed. I was through. Over the hill.

The truth is, changing light bulbs is the only male chore
left to me around the house. I have always regarded changing
light bulbs as a job that requires exquisite physical balance, a
respect for electricity, good hands and a certain amount of
engineering intuition.

I don't say that my wife, or any other woman, doesn't have
these skills; but there is the added element of danger. As the ad

implies, balancing on a chair while trying to change a light bulb is a risky business.

The chair may slide out from under you. Or you may lose your balance and fall. With your head turned up toward a ceiling fixture, and your arms raised, you may become dizzy.

Now and then I have found my wife trying to change a bulb by herself. She invariably uses a chair, though I have told her and told her that one must use a ladder, for safety's sake.

I always say, "What are you doing?"

She says, "I am changing this light bulb. It's been out for two weeks."

The implication is that she's not only quite capable of changing the bulb herself, but that I have been negligent of my duty in not changing it for two weeks.

I always instruct her to get down from the chair, and assure her that I will change the bulb immediately.

There are two reasons for this:

One, I don't want her to fall and break a leg or a hip. I would be absolutely helpless without her, since the only thing that would get done around the house would be the changing of light bulbs.

I would have nothing to eat, I would have no ironed shirts, and I would have no one to put out the trash barrels.

Two, if she changed bulbs, there would be nothing left for me to do.

In my hardier years I did concrete work. I built for the ages. In the beginning I didn't know that one could fill a pour with empty beer cans, stones and other debris, to lighten it and to save concrete.

Consequently, the steps I built from the front porch down to the sidewalk are solid concrete. I mixed it all with a shovel in a wheelbarrow, and poured it into forms I had built myself. It will never break, erode or slide.

I also built a beautiful curving downhill walk from the service porch to the front sidewalk. I swept the fresh concrete with a broom to make it slip-proof and give it an attractive texture.

Since then we have lost our milkman, who was the only reason for the walk. Our back door has been permanently locked for years. But that walk is my masterpiece. If we ever sell the house it will add $5,000 to the price.

I also built concrete steps from the upper level of our back-yard to the lower level, 12 steps with two landings. Solid as the Lincoln Memorial. Each step is bound to the next with steel brackets. My steps will never break up or slide. After the Big One has done us in, and archeologists are sifting through the debris of Mt. Washington a century or two from now, they will find those steps and wonder at the determination, ingenuity and integrity of 20th-Century man.

But I haven't done concrete since my disk slipped. I have never been much good at plumbing or carpentry, and, except for changing light bulbs, I don't fool with electricity at all.

So there isn't a lot I can do to prove that I'm still the man of the house, unless that term has been outmoded by the women's liberation movement.

I am very good at light bulbs.

I say it takes engineering intuition. When you are unscrewing a ceiling globe, for example, you have to remember that the screws on the far side of the globe must be screwed out clockwise, not counterclockwise as with those on your own side. It takes experience to get that straight.

We keep a large supply of bulbs in the linen closet, and whenever a bulb burns out, I get right on the job. At least in a week or two. You have to get yourself mentally organized to change a light bulb.

So I am not about to send away for any light bulbs that are

guaranteed to last 60,000 hours, or 20 years, whichever comes first.

Technology is not going to obsolete me.

Washing His Hands
of Her New Laundry Room

Wednesday, January 16, 1991

"WHY HAVEN'T YOU written anything about how happy we are with our new work rooms?" my wife asked the other day.

I reminded her that I had promised not to complain about our remodeling project once we started it. I had used every argument at my command to avoid it in the first place.

I argued that it would be too expensive; that we didn't need it; that it would disrupt our lives; that it would not add its cost to the value of the house.

Every one of those arguments was sound, and now, seven months after we started, they are still sound. I pointed out that we had raised two sons in our house with two bedrooms and one bath, and now, with our sons long gone and both of us near retirement, she wanted four bedrooms and three baths.

The idea seemed so ill-advised to me that I really thought she would see the light. She was adamant. She wanted to press ahead. In the end I caved in. I have reasons for wanting her to have what she wants.

We are now in our eighth month of construction. It is no small project. We are adding two workrooms (or bedrooms), a service porch and breakfast room, and a bath, and we are enlarging my old converted-garage den into a dining room that wouldn't be out of place in the Hearst Castle.

I am not complaining about the amount of time it is taking. Our contractor, Keith Rogers, is on the ball and solicitous of our discomfort. Remodeling is inevitably a slow business. One encounters unforeseen problems. Workmen are not always available when the job is ready for them. Then we had the holidays.

What troubles me now is the change the new space is working in our lives. The two workrooms are a new wing, over the garage. They were finished first, and we have moved into them, so to speak.

I admit that my new room is great. It is large and bright, with one big picture window above the street (you can see a part of the County Hospital as well as our neighbor's trash cans) and another looking out on our swimming pool and the Self Realization Fellowship on top of the hill.

I have become quite accustomed to it. My computer is installed and many of my books are in the built-in shelves. I find it very pleasant to read by the picture window. I consider the change benign, and that my life will be the better for it.

The change in my wife's life is something else. In obtaining her long-awaited service porch, she has also acquired a washing machine and dryer; also a super-quiet dishwasher.

For years we have been taking our dirty clothes out to the laundry. It did a perfectly good job. I couldn't see why she wanted to revert to washing our clothes herself. She took two weeks off from work and spent most of it washing clothes and household articles. She has washed every dirty piece in the house, and some that weren't dirty. She has washed my blanket, my robe and my Windbreaker, not to mention my socks, underwear and shirts.

She has washed a robe of hers that was blackened with newsprint. "See how clean it is?" she asked, holding it up proudly. She reminds me of those housewives in the ads in the women's magazines, bragging about their household machines.

She has moved her paperwork to her new room, along with her ironing board and her TV set. She spends hours ironing the clothes she has washed. Already her new desk and her library table are covered with bills, letters, catalogues and junk mail. I hope that means that the dining room table will at last be clear, and that, for the first time in years, we can have guests to dinner.

What worries me is her apparent regression. I would not call her a radical feminist, but she surely was a liberated woman, even if she did cook all our microwave dinners. She has a management job, she has control of our bank account, she has her own savings, she has a car, she has a handsome wardrobe, she has season tickets to the Philharmonic, the Mark Taper and the Theater Center, she subscribes to the Book-of-the-Month Club, and she has a devoted and helpful husband.

What I want to know is how could a woman with all those advantages suddenly become enamored of washing and ironing clothes? It isn't that a washing machine is a captivating or challenging toy, like a computer. No, I think it's simply that she likes washing clothes and resents not having had a washing machine all those years.

If only one knew what they wanted.

From Intensive Care to Dance Floor Flair

Thursday, June 14, 1990

I FOUND OUT the other day what it would be like not having my wife; I don't think I have the mettle for it.

She woke me up at about 12:30 in the morning. She said she had a terrible pain in her chest. She was moaning and crying out and bending over. Her usual reaction to any indisposition is embarrassment. She doesn't like to think that anything could be wrong with her.

I was alarmed. I decided to wake up our doctor. He said to call the paramedics and have her taken to Huntington Memorial Hospital.

I called 911. A few minutes later a fire engine came. Then the ambulance. One of the ambulance men looked familiar. Big, good-looking man named Jim Goldsworthy. He said, "I remember you."

He was one of the crew that had taken me to County Hospital when I had my "arrhythmic episode." He said, "I didn't think you were going to make it." I almost didn't.

They took my wife away in the ambulance. I followed in my car. By the time I parked and went into the emergency unit she was already in bed with tubes in her arms.

The duty doctor, Dr. Roy Antelyes, said it was too early for a diagnosis. He said he was going to call our doctor, Tom Callister. I hated to think of that poor man having to get out of bed and get dressed, but of course that's his job.

Meanwhile, the duty nurse, Melanie Crowley, was being very cheerful. I don't know how they can be cheerful in those places.

Dr. Callister arrived and began examining my wife. He said they would have to make some extensive tests. It would take time. She told him the annual dinner-dance of her counseling center was Friday night (the next day) and she *had* to be there.

The doctor shook his head. "No way," he said.

He said the cardiologist would examine her in the morning.

I got home at 3:30 and went to sleep about 4. At 7:30 she called. "Were you asleep?" she asked.

Not only was I worried about her the next day, but I felt guilty when I had to do her chores. She is really overworked. First, I had to feed the cats. She feeds five wild cats every morning. They gather on the front porch, whining and screeching. I hadn't the slightest idea how to feed them. I found a large can of cat food and divided it between two bowls and put them out on the porch and withdrew my hands quickly. If that wasn't enough for them, let the beggars starve.

Then I had to feed the dog. Then I had to make coffee. She had given me a list of last-minute chores pertaining to the dinner-dance. I had to go to Supervisor Ed Edelman's office to pick up a resolution. I parked at The Times, walked up hill to Temple and Grand, and found Edelman's office on the eighth floor at the end of a long hall.

Then I had to deliver the resolution to the Southern California Counseling Center, of which she is administrative director. She believes that the dinner-dance can not take place without her. Everyone was stunned to hear that she was in the hospital. She is not supposed to get sick.

Then I had to keep a date to talk to the Friends of the Center at a luncheon in Beverly Hills. By then I was a nervous wreck. Then I drove to the hospital. Because of new construction, the hospital is almost inaccessible. I had to park in a new parking structure and take a shuttle to the hospital itself. I carried a bouquet given me by the luncheon hostess. The hospital is a labyrinth. It took me 20 minutes to find her room, and it was guarded like Ft. Knox. She was in intensive care.

She was watching a soap opera. She said they hadn't found any heart damage but they had to do more tests. She said she was going to get out. I said, "No way."

The next morning she called me and said to stand by. She was going to get out. I was afraid she was simply going to put on her robe and escape. "Don't do anything foolish," I told her.

I had to feed the dog and the cats again. I was really beginning to appreciate her. The phone kept ringing. A deliveryman hammered on the door. Later she called and said to come and get her. She had talked her way out. She told me to bring her some underwear, a dress and some shoes. I found the designated articles and stuffed them in a shopping bag and drove to the hospital.

She was ready to go. "You're not going to the dance," I said hopefully. "You bet I am," she said.

I was frazzled out, but I had to dress in my tux and escort her. They think she had a hiatus hernia, whatever that is.

CHAPTER 10

Semiretirement or Just Muddling About?

He'll Continue to Be the Best
That He Can Be

Monday, December 23, 1991

HAVING WRITTEN more columns than Pete Rose has hits, I am accepting the inevitable and retiring from my Monday-through-Thursday column at the end of this month.

For those who may miss me, I am happy to say that I will continue to write one column a week.

The Times did not urge me to take this step; in fact, I have had nothing from The Times, for more than 30 years, but hands-off support.

I simply feel that I have worked hard enough long enough and hope that I may enjoy some relief from my arduous schedule. My wife is afraid I will do nothing but drink beer and watch television. She may be right.

I suspect, though, that writing one column a week will be almost as hard as writing five, which I did for 20 years. Before that, I did three a week for 10 years. I will think about it each week until it is done and then, at once, I will start thinking about the next one, which will be coming toward me like a train on a track.

I do not think, either, that having to write only one will make the product any better. Every column I have ever written was the best I could do, at that time. Many, of course, were dreadful; but the reason one writes a regular column is that one must. The deadline is, finally, the motivator.

Marilyn Hudson, co-hostess of the Round Table West, once said that writing a daily newspaper column is like making love to a nymphomaniac. When you're finished, and think you're through, you have to start all over again.

A column is an essay. It usually examines one idea, or notion, which it turns over briefly and then abandons. A columnist hopes to be provocative or, if he's lucky, funny. Often he is dismissed as peddling trivia. I never thought of anything I wrote as trivia.

I have often been asked, "What is your column about?" My answer is that it is about being me and living in Los Angeles. Consequently, I hoped, it would be about everybody who lives in Los Angeles.

E. B. White once said that "the essayist is sustained by the childish belief that everything he thinks about, everything that happens to him, is of general interest."

Recently a reader wrote that he had counted 35 *I*'s in one of my columns. He said that was enough. He wasn't reading me anymore. I'm sure I've used *I* more than 35 times in one column.

In a review of White's collected essays, Richard Freedman said, "The greatest gift of the essayistic mind: to extract a momentous truth from the most seemingly trivial event or artifact."

If my material has sometimes seemed trivial, I assure you that it was chosen in the hope of yielding up a momentous truth, though I have no doubt that such truths usually escaped the reader.

When Russell Baker told his editor he was going to quit writing his Sunday column for the New York Times, the editor told him to write a final column explaining why. "Are you asking me to abandon good taste by talking about myself?" Baker asked.

"Then," he said, "I thought: Why not? Abandoning good taste is one of the things newspapermen do best, and talking about myself is one of my favorite pastimes."

After 15 years, Baker put his finger on the problem:

"Fifteen years, more than 700 columns of about 800 words per column makes about 560,000 words of what was supposed to be inventive prose. Nobody can be that inventive."

When Charles Champlin retired after 13 years as The Times' film critic and critic at large, he calculated that he had written more than 2.2 million words—"a sobering thought on a lovely spring morning."

In 30 years I have probably written more than 5 million words. Some philosopher once said that nobody had more than three good ideas in a lifetime. To write 5 million words, I have had to do a lot of recycling of my three good ideas.

I cannot leave my career without thanking the thousands of readers who have supported me over the years. Their letters sustained me. Most of my columns were drawn from them. I read every one. I intended to answer every one, but I could not keep up. To this day, I have cardboard boxes full of letters I hope to answer.

To those that did not receive an answer I want to say that your letters were read and appreciated, every one, even those that said they wished I would drop dead. Sometimes those made the best columns.

I hope, when I'm writing only once a week, for the Monday paper, you won't forsake me.

She Really Knows How to Hurt a Guy

Monday, October 19, 1992

THERE ARE HAZARDS in semi-retirement. Whereas I wrote five columns a week for 20 years (and three for another 10) I am now reduced to one a week.

That does give me some time to muddle about in.

So far, that's what I've been doing with my extra time. Muddling. I have taken a few young women out to lunch, but I sense that they didn't find my company scintillating. I may have to give that up.

I have thought about finishing my novel—"Summer's End." But so far I have written only the first six words. "It was the end of summer."

I have subscribed to the New York Times, so that I have both the New York Times and the Los Angeles Times to read every morning. If you do a thorough job it takes half a day.

We have season tickets to the Philharmonic and the Mark Taper Forum, so several evenings are devoted to cultural pursuits.

That leaves the afternoons and most of the evenings. And that's where the deadly specter of television comes in.

I have never been addicted to daytime television. I didn't have time. But lately I have found myself watching it more and more. I never watch the talk shows. They are mostly about sex. I like sex, but I'd rather see it as fiction in a movie than in the real life confession of some adulterous wife.

Now and then I watch a movie. I especially like the old movies shown on AMC, and also Westerns. Watching an old Western is a good way to spend an afternoon, and my wife, being at work, is none the wiser.

In the evening it is our custom to watch a movie—usually sex and violence—while eating a microwave dinner on trays. My wife doesn't like it when I say we eat microwave dinners, pointing out that she often cooks dinners from fresh ingredients. True. But I am not picky about what I eat. I never complain about microwave dinners. If I really cared I'd cook dinner myself.

But I've been slipping. I spent two weeks in front of the

tube during the U.S. Tennis Open. Lately I've had to watch football: College on Saturdays, pros on Sundays.

Last Monday I had a dilemma. I was watching Monday Night Football, a habit I've had for years, and one that my wife excuses, but I turned away from it to watch "Once Upon a Time in the West," a Western that runs for 3 hours and 30 minutes.

"What's that?" my wife asked.

I told her. "It's got three stars," I said. "Henry Fonda plays a villain."

"What about football?"

I told her I was taping it in the bedroom. "That means you'll watch it tomorrow," she said. I said yes, of course.

She said, "You're watching more television than a school kid."

I was stung. I am very sensitive to her innuendoes about the way I spend my time. I especially didn't like being compared with a school kid in my television habits. I'm told the average school kid watches 28 hours of TV every week. That's scandalous and I certainly didn't want to be in that category.

I turned off both sets. The game and the Western. "What are you doing?" she asked rather nervously.

"I'm giving up television," I said. "I don't like being compared to a school kid. From now on, if you want to watch a movie at night, you can pick it out yourself. I'm no longer going to do our programming."

That evening we ate dinner in the dining room, for the first time in months. It happened to be lamb chops that she had prepared herself.

We began talking about this and that. It seemed we had a lot to catch up on.

"I don't know when we've talked this much at dinner," she said.

It was the same thing the next night. I didn't watch TV during the day, and that night I didn't suggest a movie. We ate in the dining room again.

I hadn't realized how much television was stealing away our lives. I made us each a vodka tonic; actually, they were doubles. We became very talkative. After dinner my wife caught up on her paper work and I did some reading.

So far I haven't cracked yet. I have a great deal of negative strength. When I say I'm not going to do something I don't do it.

I did watch "Hunter" reruns every weekday. I was waiting for a rerun of that unusual episode in which the cop partners, Hunter and DeeDee McCall, go to bed together. I'd heard about it. By an improbable coincidence, it turned up just the other day. They ended up confessing to a police psychiatrist.

That finishes me with "Hunter."

L.A. Birdman Sighted
in La Canada Flintridge

Wednesday, December 11, 1991

SUNDAY MORNING, my wife and I got up at 6 o'clock for the annual Jack and Denny Smith bird walk at Descanso Gardens.

It was raining. My wife said, "You think they'd have a bird walk in the rain?"

She telephoned Karen Johnson, who leads the walk, and asked if she was going on with it. Johnson said she would be there, even if she was the only one.

When we left the house the rain had stopped. The air was

damp and cold. Driving up Linda Vista Drive and then Berkshire Avenue, through La Canada Flintridge we felt that it was the best of all possible worlds.

There were more joggers than cars in the streets. Along Berkshire, mansions of various architectural styles sat back behind lawns, oaks and sycamores. BMWs and Mercedes-Benzes stood in curved driveways. Newspapers lay where they had been tossed.

Only about 25 birders were gathered inside the gate at Descanso for the walk. They were a motley bunch, in warm coats and caps. Most carried binoculars and bird books. Johnson made a brief talk and called on me. I said birders were an odd lot, but not so odd as to want to hear a talk on a cold and rainy morning.

The bird walk is not as old an institution as the Tournament of Roses, but it has been going on more years than anyone, including Johnson, can remember. It was started after I sighted a common grackle in my back yard, an event so rare (in fact unprecedented) that it made me something of a celebrity in birding circles. On some past Sundays more than 200 birders had attended.

We plodded off over the damp leafy paths through groves of oaks and sycamores, Johnson leading. "Varied thrush!" she suddenly called out. We were galvanized. "It's very rare here," she said. "Maybe one a year. It's a good omen."

Birds began appearing almost too rapidly to identify. "We've got a mockingbird on the right," called Johnson. "There's a robin in the oak tree," a woman shouted. "Ruby-crowned kinglet!"... "Black phoebe in the rosebush!"

Johnson pointed to a flock of gray birds circling above the trees. "Cedar waxwings," she said. I knew cedar waxwings. They used to flock in our cotoneaster bush in the front yard and get drunk on fermented berries. A very human bird.

Various species began to pop up. Fat California quail waddled across the path. Yellow-rumped warblers. Someone spied a hermit thrush. Anna's hummingbirds hovered in a great oak. A red-tailed hawk. Cooper's hawk.

My wife said there seemed to be more birds than ever before. I said there were no more birds; it was just that, there being fewer people, instead of tailing off at the end of the group to socialize, we were actually bird-watching.

A large bird with a long neck soared overhead. Someone identified it, correctly, according to Johnson, as a cormorant. Strange place for a sea bird, I thought.

From the bird station above the pond we looked down on numerous water birds, including a school of ring-tail ducks that were just sitting there. They looked like sitting ducks.

"Look at the squirrels," my wife said, pointing to three fat squirrels playing around a gnarled oak tree. "We don't report squirrels," I told her. "Only birds."

Finally the perennial great blue heron showed up, flapping low over the pond and taking refuge in a bush. The heron had never disappointed us, year after year. Johnson said it was probably the same bird.

"Scrub jay," Johnson cried. Actually, I have always held that scrub jays should be blue jays, because they're jays and they're blue. This bird is far too beautiful to be called a scrub. But in this notion I am ridiculed by the erudite Hank Childs, birdman of Upland. He says the blue jay is an altogether different bird.

I suppose I have a lot to learn about birds. But I do know a grackle when I see one.

Mugger Seems Trivial
Next to a Vodka Tonic

Monday, June 28, 1993

S Y C A M O R E   G R O V E is a small park at the foot of our hill. It is named for its growth of large, old sycamore trees. Eucalyptus and oaks are also abundant. It has a carpet of thick grass. It is circled by an uneven asphalt walk.

It was the site for many years of state picnics. Hundreds of out-of-staters met in its shade to eat barbecued beef and talk of home. My wife and I have driven by it hundreds of times. When we were younger, we played tennis on its courts. But in recent years we had hardly noticed the park.

Finally, looking for a place to take a daily rehabilitative walk, we drove down to look it over. It hadn't changed much. There was a volleyball court, two tennis courts, restrooms, the usual park trappings.

We drove down in the late afternoon, when the day was beginning to cool and the park's people were beginning to come out. They came in every kind of vehicle. Pickups, vans, sedans, bicycles—mostly older models. Pickups disgorged whole families. Some men sat alone at the curb, drinking beer.

The sidewalk along Figueroa Street looked like a good place to walk. It ran about a quarter of a mile. We decided to walk it one way and back, rather than circling the park. For months I had been going to the Pasadena Athletic Club three mornings a week, doing a light workout on the bicycle and walking half a mile on the track. That would be too strenuous for me now.

We told a friend of our plan. He said, "Be careful. That park can be dangerous." Indeed, I had read in the local newspaper of several robberies and muggings in Highland Park. It was no longer the peaceful small town it had been when I lived here as a boy.

It was also multicultural now. Most of the population were Latinos. Koreans owned the liquor stores and other small businesses. Occasionally there was a shooting on the street. Graffiti abounded.

"You'd better not take your purse," I told my wife, thinking it would be an open invitation to a purse snatcher. The first time we went, she left her purse and I left my billfold at home. That made it awkward when we wanted to stop at the market for tonic water after the walk. I have become addicted to a single vodka tonic before dinner. Somehow, evidently a result of my ordeal, I have lost my taste for wine. Vodka hits the spot. As Herb Caen says, it's vitamin V.

Several entrepreneurs were parked along the street. One of them offered mangoes for sale, another watermelons.

Now and then a boy walked by with a pushcart of ice cream. I wondered how they could make a living with such meager sales as the park must afford. They all seemed cheerful. They smiled. They said hello.

We soon got into the spirit. We said hello to everybody. Numerous small children swarmed around us on bicycles. Pregnant women walked the paths. A pickup volleyball game was going on. There were at least five soccer games. Teen-age boys were playing hockey on the tennis court. Numerous young people, sparsely dressed, lay stretched out on the grass. An old man threw a ball for his dog to fetch.

We wanted to buy a watermelon from a man who had a load of them in his pickup. But we didn't have any money. The next day my wife brought her purse. It was a bright yellow and the size of a briefcase. "Don't you have a less conspicuous one?" I asked her. "I didn't think," she said. It is her belief that nothing bad can happen to her.

As it turned out, nothing did. Manly joggers passed us by without a flicker of their eyelids. A man who looked like a pirate said, "Have a nice day" as he trotted by.

I prevailed on her the next day not to take her purse. But a crisis developed. It occurred to her as we were driving down the hill that we were out of vodka. That meant I would miss my nightly fix. We were obliged to go home and get her purse after all.

The danger of being held up seemed trivial beside the loss of a comforting vodka tonic. Besides, how can you take part in the park's economy without money? She has been carrying her purse ever since. The only danger we have sensed so far is the danger of being clipped by a kid whizzing past on a bicycle. They love close encounters.

The truth is, we are no more likely to be held up in Sycamore Grove than we are in the parking entrance of the Beverly Wilshire. And one thing you can't do at the Beverly Wilshire: You can't buy fresh watermelons.

Bag Lady Leaves Him
With Mayo on His Face

Monday, January 6, 1992

I WAS ABOUT to enter Langer's Delicatessen, at 7th and Alvarado, when I was approached by a street woman. She may have been 50, maybe 30. She bore the signs of wear and tear. She was dressed in a soiled blouse and blue jeans. She was scrawny. Her movements were quick.

She said, "Sir, could you help me out?"

I opened my billfold and gave her a dollar. She thanked me, acting surprised and grateful.

I went into the restaurant and had a patty melt and a beer. I've been dropping in at Langer's for lunch now and then for many years, usually by myself. It is an old-fashioned deli. The waitresses are no longer young but they call me *dearie.* I couldn't remember that I had ever been hit up by a mendicant outside it before.

When I left the restaurant the woman suddenly appeared again. "Sir," she said, evidently pushing her luck, "could you buy me a hamburger? I'm awful hungry."

I hesitated. I knew I was being taken. But she probably *was* hungry. I started walking. She fell in beside me. We came to a little hamburger shop. I knew I should go in with her and buy the hamburger, make sure she ate it. But I felt diffident about that.

I opened my billfold and took out two ones. They were the only ones I had. I gave them to her.

"Hamburgers are $3," she said.

I saw a sign in the window. Hamburgers were indeed $3.

I was in for $2, I might as well go all the way. I took out a five, thinking I would go in the shop, buy the hamburger and collect my change. She said, "Give me the five and I'll give you back the $2."

I knew there was something wrong with that, but I wasn't sure what. As I have said before, I am not good at numbers. I gave her the five, thinking she could buy the hamburger with it and give me the change.

She looked quickly at the five and the two and evidently decided that she was not likely to improve on such luck. She darted into the street, doing a little victory dance, like a wide receiver after scoring a touchdown.

"Give me back my $2!" I shouted, simultaneously realizing that I was miscalculating somehow. She mocked me jubilantly and darted up the street. She was too fleet for me to catch, and even if I had caught her, I couldn't see myself wrestling her to the sidewalk and extracting my money from her fists.

I stood there trying to figure it out. She not only had the $2, she also had the five. So, counting the dollar I had given her in the first place, she had $8 of my money. Not a bad score for a street person.

I was angrier at myself than at her. After all, she had just been trying to make a buck. I was dismayed by my own stupidity. I ought not be allowed out on the streets alone, I thought.

I walked back to my car, dejected.

I have been thinking of going back to 7th and Alvarado and looking for her. Surely she wouldn't have abandoned such a lucrative corner. But if I did find her, I thought, what would I do?

Would I say, "Hey, you stole $7 from me," and demand my money back? Don't be silly. She would simply pretend not to recognize me. Would I look around for a cop? Don't be silly. What cop would believe I could be that dumb? Besides, I wouldn't want to admit to a cop that I *had* been that dumb.

Keeping Up With the Flow to Cambria

Monday, August 30, 1993

MY WIFE AND I have returned from a three-day holiday in Cambria, a Central California village where the pines meet the sea. Our son Curt rented a house for a week and invited us to spend some time with him and his family.

We had spent two of the last three months in a hospital, and thought the trip might do us good. I wasn't sure spending some time with three children would be restful, but they were exemplary, partly because Curt had the foresight to buy them a 550-piece jigsaw puzzle, which tied them down for two afternoons.

I spent most of my time reading "The Neon Jungle," by John D. MacDonald. My wife pointed out that I had read it at least two times before. Why aren't there any writers like John D. MacDonald anymore?

The trip up had been glorious. My wife drove her Maxima, at her usual average speed of 80 m.p.h. When I suggested she might be going too fast, she said, "I'm just keeping up with the traffic flow." It was true. Even at 80, we were being passed.

The drive up California 101, from Ventura to San Luis Obispo, offers a beautiful panorama of Central California, a refreshment to the spirit. The road winds through hills and pastures, past wonderful old barns with corrugated roofs. The grassy hills are round and plump, like Rubens' nudes. They are dotted with brown cows, sometimes solitary, sometimes in congregations. In their idleness, they seem to slow down time, a mockery to our speeding cars.

We skirted a number of small towns of the kind that many Angelenos are fleeing to. Santa Maria was once called the ideal American town, and I believe it was the setting for the 1946 movie, "The Best Years of Our Lives," a story of servicemen returning after World War II.

Somewhere near Santa Maria, we picked up a Bakersfield station that played nothing but country music. Bakersfield, sometimes called Nashville West, is the Western home of country music. It has an aura. Anywhere its radio signal reaches, you are going to be inundated with those poignant laments about love, betrayal and redemption.

Mile after mile we picked up those lovelorn lyrics:

If tomorrow I found one more chance to begin, I'd love you all over again....

Somewhere above Ventura, Curt called on my wife's car phone. He wanted to know where we were. We told him. "Then you'll be here in a couple of hours," he said. I asked him how he figured. "Because Mom drives 80 miles an hour," he said.

I can't go wrong loving you....

There's no time to waste between the cradle and the grave....

Beyond Santa Maria, the Bakersfield station began to fade, but I caught this last lament:

All the gold in California is in a bank in the middle of Beverly Hills in somebody else's name....

A few miles south of Cambria, on California 1, we pulled off at Harmony. It may be the smallest town in America. It didn't seem to have grown any since we last saw it a few years ago. A sign said "Harmony, population 18." There was a creamery, a post office, a pasta factory, some art shops and two or three houses. I decided it was too small for me. Not enough excitement.

We reached Cambria in the two hours our son had predicted. The house was a three-story rustic, with decks overlooking the sea. I got out my book and quickly adjusted to the pace. I was spared the humiliation of losing to my grandsons in Scrabble, as I had done before, by their commitment to the jigsaw puzzle.

My son was talking about retiring and moving to some place like Cambria. I couldn't believe it. My son talking about retiring already. Why, I was not really retired yet myself. Of course, he would have to wait until his children were out of school, and the oldest is only 16. She wants to go to college, but not in Los Angeles and not to a women's college. She's thinking Harvard.

Whenever I travel, I always read the local newspapers. In the Cambria paper, I found at least two good reasons why it was not a good place to retire. One, the Cambria and Cayucos school district was out of money and had to drop a teacher, give up after-school sports and curtail its school-library services. What else was new?

Also, they had found a rabid bat in San Luis Obispo County. One thing we don't have in Los Angeles is rabid bats. Or do we? God knows we have plenty of rabid people.

The main thing to remember is that there's no time to waste between the cradle and the grave.

Adios to Gomez
and Their Baja Mansion

Sunday, July 8, 1990

A L L good things must end.

Lately, many people have asked me why I no longer write of my friend Romulo Gomez and the house he built for us in Baja California.

I think it is time for me to report that my wife and I have sold the house. We found that we were not using it often enough, and a house that is not lived in tends to deteriorate. We have sold it to two young couples who, we hope, will enjoy it as much as we did.

It had been a great experience for us; it was something we shared; perhaps it helped hold us together.

It was rather a bold undertaking in the first place. A friend at The Times had told me about Gomez and the land he had for lease to Americans at La Bocana—the mouth of the Santo Tomas River, below Ensenada. My friend thought we might like to lease some land and have Gomez build a house for us. I told him he was crazy.

That night at dinner, I told my wife about it, laughing at the idiocy of it, and put it out of my mind. Months later, we drove down to Indio for the date festival, but found that we were two weeks early. I said good, we could go home and rest. My wife said we could drive on down to Baja and look at that property that was for lease.

I told her I didn't even remember the man's name. "Gomez," she said. "It was Gomez."

So you can see that it was her adventure from the start. We drove on down to Ensenada, spent the night, and the next day drove on without a map; all I remembered was that Gomez's store was at the mouth of the Santo Tomas River, and that the river valley was about 25 miles south of Ensenada.

We crossed the winding highway through the mountains and came to a green river valley. A sign said Bahia Santo Tomas. It was an incredibly bad road, even for Baja—narrow and rocky and full of holes. It crossed the riverbed several times, making me wonder what the trip would be like when the river was up.

We passed an adobe schoolhouse, some adobe houses, a few farms and a beautiful oak grove. Finally, after 18 miles of rough going, we came out at the bay, and there was a little store. I left my wife in the car and went in. It had shelves of ketchup and beans and other staples, and beer on ice. A girl was sweeping out. I asked if she knew a man named Gomez.

"*Momento*," she said. She went into the kitchen at the back. In a moment a man emerged. He was a tall, good-looking

Mexican, somewhat older and fleshier than I. He wore a straw field hat. He said, in a melodious voice, "I am Gomez."

It turned out to be a fateful meeting.

Gomez drove us out on a beautiful marine terrace overlooking Santo Tomas Bay. Porpoises flashed in the bay. Pelicans flew over it in formation. To the north, the rocky Santo Tomas Point gleamed like obsidian. There were only two other houses in view—both orange brick with red tile roofs. We were enchanted. There were no streets, no stakes, no lots. Only a road of two ruts leading from Gomez's store to the fishing camp on the point. We picked out a site.

Gomez said, "You like this lot?"

We said yes, we did.

Gomez said, "This is your lot."

He drove us back to the store, and his wife, Delia, cooked us a marvelous breakfast of *chiles rellenos* and fresh lobster from the bay.

I gave Gomez a check for $100, and we sealed the bargain with a shot of tequila.

In Baja, any deal that is sealed with tequila is binding.

That was more than 20 years ago.

Three months later, we drove back to give Gomez some more money and a plan I had drawn. I told him to go ahead. It was another three months before we came back. He was building our house but not on our lot. It was in the middle of the rutted road. I asked him, "Gomez, why are you building the house in the middle of the road?"

He said, "Because the road has the best view."

We were to become familiar with that kind of logic. Months later Gomez and I were sitting on the front porch of our still-unfinished mansion, as he called it. It was considerably larger than I'd planned it. Gomez was explaining why, under Mexican law, we could not have a deed.

I asked him, "Then how will we know it's ours?"

He said, "I will give you the key."

I had always told him I would not consider the house finished until the toilet was in. He called us from Tijuana one day and told us the house was finished. The toilet was in. We rushed down to La Bocana and threw open our front door. The toilet was sitting in the living room.

The house had taken more than a year to build. We loved it, and my wife loved it even more than I did, but she has always been more adventurous than I. Many weekends, incredibly, when I was otherwise engaged, she drove down to the house after work on Friday nights, alone, driving the last 18 miles of horrible, unlighted, unpaved Baja road, and arrived at midnight. Sunday night she drove home. She spent most of her time housecleaning. One such weekend, she fell on the rocks above the seashore and broke her leg. Fortunately, two neighbors were with her. As soon as the cast was off, she drove down again.

But over the years the road became longer; thicker traffic had made the trip more tedious. The long delay at the border coming home was harder to bear. We realized finally that we had not gone down to the house for two years. It was either sell or surrender it to the mice.

That morning when we first agreed with Gomez to lease the lot, we discussed our fantasy on the way home in a sort of delirium. We agreed that, however bad things might go, we would never blame each other. Things were often very bad; but we never blamed each other. I think, in that sense, that house was one of the most important ventures in our lives.

People often ask me if Gomez is still alive. Sadly, his wife, Delia, died a few years ago; she was a wonderful woman. But Gomez is still alive and he has not changed. He is as exasperating as ever. [Editor's note: Mr. Gomez died of cancer in

October, 1994.]

He has a code. He does not admit what does not need admitting. Thus, when a fire destroyed our bathroom cabinet, he never admitted that it was started accidentally by one of his sons. More recently, when our ancient Servel gas refrigerator finally stopped working, he did not admit that another of his sons was trying to hook a gas line to a new water heater and accidentally hooked it up to the refrigerator instead. Of course, he knows that I know, but we do not discuss it. Friends must respect each other's sensitivities.

American entrepreneurs keep scheming to develop the little fishing camp on the point of the bay into a glitzy resort, but their dreams invariably subside in the Baja sand.

No, I never found out whether Gomez really owns the land. Perhaps the new owners will.

Angelenos Would Rather Gripe Than Switch

Sunday, May 28, 1989

A s a r e c e n t Times poll showed, almost half of all Angelenos are so disenchanted with Los Angeles that they have thought of moving out.

On the other hand, few do. Some have decamped to Northern California, Oregon and other nearby states, but their numbers hardly constitute a land rush.

One reason we are reluctant to locate elsewhere, I suspect, is that we are afraid that our reputation as laid-back, amoral, greedy and rude will have preceded us, and we may find the natives hostile.

Our minorities may contribute to our overcrowding, but they are also victims of it. They might prosper in smaller communities elsewhere, but they may fear being ostracized not only because they are Angelenos, but also because they are minorities.

Seattle Times columnist Tom Kelly wrote recently about "California jerks" who sell their inflated equities and move to the Northwest, where they drive up housing prices and otherwise disturb the equanimity of life.

Noting that he came to Seattle from Santa Monica only 14 years ago, Kelly wonders whether there is a "statute of limitations" on California jerks, or whether, once a jerk, always a jerk.

He suggests that California jerks can ease their entry by making a few intermediate stops. If you spend a year in Arkansas, for example, and a couple in Iowa, you can really be "from" Iowa. On the other hand, newcomers from the nearby states of Idaho, Montana and Oregon are simply "neighbors, and get a free ride."

I can understand why Kelly resents Californians coming into Washington and ruining the ecology of that wonderland (he is especially worried about the San Juan Islands). But, of course, this is a free country, not Russia; Americans can move anywhere they like.

I don't like to use that old taunt, "If you don't like it here, why don't you go back where you came from?" The Statue of Liberty sheds her grace on all of us. "Give me your tired, your poor, your huddled masses..." and all that. But, also, the door opens both ways. If Los Angeles is too crowded, too polluted, too dangerous, then why not try Tungsten, Nev., near Rye Patch Reservoir and the Humboldt River?

Several years ago, I visited Good Thunder, Minn., at the invitation of the local publisher. The town was dying. Its young people had gravitated to the big city. It was wide-open for exploitation, with rows of empty storefronts and plenty of cheap houses. Why don't some of us migrate to Good Thunder and bring its economy back?

There is plenty of space out there. What's the matter with Medicine Bow, Wyoming, near the Freezeout Mountains? Why not try Hardin, Mont., near the Custer battlefield? There must be opportunities in Mountain Home, Idaho, near the Mountain Home Air Force Base. What about Syracuse, Utah, on the Great Salt Lake?

Bill Seavey makes a living out of helping city people relocate in small towns. He is president of EMIGRANTS (Endangered Metropolitan Inhabitants/Growth opponents Resettling in Arcadian Neighborhoods, Towns and Suburbs—perhaps the longest almost-acronym in existence).

In response to a previous column of mine on moving out, Seavey said: "I, too, agree that there are wide-open spaces in the West, and I'm obviously not alone. But convincing people to consider relocation is a tough nut. I maintain that there is no *official* encouragement, and that's part of the problem. People need support."

Maybe people longing to breathe free *should* get some official support. It might be helpful if the Greater Los Angeles Chamber of Commerce opened a Back to the Sticks desk to advise those who want to go elsewhere. They'd probably get plenty of cooperation from places such as Buffalo Gap, Tex. (There is also a Buffalo Gap in South Dakota, if you're interested.)

Curse it as they will, most people are not likely to leave Los Angeles. Big cities, like big celestial bodies, have more gravity than small ones. Besides, with all its faults, Los Angeles is probably the freest city in the world.

As for me, I'm staying right here until I'm shot, hit by a car or asphyxiated.

CHAPTER 11

Savoring the Present Tense Before It's Past

Delivering an Oration to a Captured Audience

Monday, June 7, 1993

I HAD NO IDEA a heart attack could be so devastating.

I went into Huntington Memorial Hospital one morning in April for what I supposed would be routine surgery (prostate, if you must know), and I have no recollection of what happened in the next few days.

When I regained my senses, I was a basket case. I had entered the hospital in fairly good shape for an old man. I could walk straight; even dance, when pressed. I had a spring in my step. I was reasonably sane.

All that was gone when I regained my self-awareness in the intensive-care unit. My legs were rubber. My sense of balance was awry. Unfortunately, my ability to speak was unimpaired.

The next few days are blank. I am dependent on reports from my relatives and other eyewitnesses for clues to my behavior in that unfortunate period.

For a time, in ICU everyone had expected me to die. In fact, I heard later, The Times was preparing my obituary. Preparedness is everything.

My wife had summoned our sons to the hospital, and they were there when things seemed the darkest. My wife had been on her feet 24 hours when they sent her home to get some rest. She took a shower and lay down. In a few minutes, she jumped out of bed, angry. She had decided to go back to the hospital and tell me not to die. When she arrived at the hospital, I had taken a turn for the better. She is convinced that her will had something to do with it.

Some time in the next few days (I have no memory of it whatsoever) I evidently delivered myself of a stunning diatribe against the hospital, loudly citing all its offenses against me as a free individual.

I protested that I was being held a prisoner, against my will. Indeed, my arms were restrained because I had been pulling out IVs and other apparatus attached to my body. I am terrified of any restraint.

I alleged that the hospital's staff should be arrested and put in prison. I said they were all felons. Unfortunately, one of my auditors was Allen Mathies, president of Huntington Hospital. Mathies is a friend of mine and a very amiable man, but his ears must have been stung by my unsolicited oration.

As I say, I do not remember a word of it. As far as I know, it never happened. However, numerous eyewitnesses testify to my prolonged protest.

I'm sure Mathies knows, being a medical man, that I was stark raving paranoid. I cannot remember a more clear-cut case of hospital dementia.

In my unrestrained assault, of course, I ignored or was unaware of the fact that the hospital was merely doing those things that its best minds considered necessary to save my life.

The greatest indignity of all, I think, must have been when they stuck a pipe down my nasal passage into my lungs. Fortunately, I wasn't aware of it or have no memory of it. Thank God.

Among my listeners were my wife and two sons, Curt and Doug. Evidently they were more embarrassed than moved by my indictment. I asked each of them in turn to drive me home. They declined. I told my older son, Curt, that he was to call the police and have the hospital staff put in jail for false imprisonment and torture. I instructed him to hire a lawyer. He said he couldn't do that. I threatened to dismiss him as my executor and to disinherit him; he was unmoved.

In desperation I turned to my daughter-in-law Jacqueline, asking her to drive me out of this dungeon of iniquity and home. She said she could not do it. It was the end.

My younger son offered a word of consolation. "Well," he said, "at least you still have your vocabulary." I guess I was lucky to have escaped with that.

A day or two later, he decided to put me to the test. "Do you know your car license number?" he asked. I happened to know it because it is so unusual. It is **YHEE OR**, which is Hebrew for "Let there be light." I had wanted **FIAT LUX**, which is Latin for "Let there be light," but it was taken. It was Rabbi Alfred Wolf, my spiritual adviser, who suggested the Hebrew, direct from Genesis.

"What kind of car do you have?" Doug asked. I couldn't remember.

Allen Mathies never appeared in my ward again during my month-long stay in his hospital. But I did receive a single pink rose in a slender vase. I hoped it was a symbol of forgiveness.

As soon as I was considered out of grave danger, I was transferred to a progressive-care unit. All the doctors and nurses in ICU must have been greatly relieved.

...Then in the Dark There Arose Such a Clatter...

Monday, June 14, 1993

I WAS STILL wobbling like a toddler when they moved me into a recovery unit at Huntington Memorial Hospital after my heart attack. My mind was still wobbly too. I kept asking the staff where all the books were. I thought I was in the Huntington Library.

In my new unit we were still regarded as subhuman, which I, at least, certainly was.

On the wall of my room was a set of **RULES**, printed in large black type.

The No. 2 rule was this: "Patients shall call the nurse for assistance out of bed until physicians and therapists deem patients safe to do so independently."

This was a sound rule, as I was soon to demonstrate. Each bed was equipped with a small electronic switch box by which a patient could turn on his television set, raise or lower his bed or call his nurse. Nurses were supposed to respond immediately to this bell, and when I used it, they did.

On the second night, though, when I was still hardly more intelligent than a marsupial, I decided I was old enough to go to the bathroom without assistance. It was rather humiliating to have to be led. I had been going to the bathroom alone for many years.

I managed to work my way out of bed and began a precarious walk toward my destination. Alas, my legs betrayed me. With a great clatter, I fell into a trap of hospital equipment. I bruised my forehead, sprained a wrist and gave one elbow an abrasion that produced a scab as big as a dollar.

I was rescued by a nurse who scolded me as if I were a small child, which, of course, I was. The next morning when I awoke I had a restraining strap around one arm, preventing me from leaving my bed, and an orange band around one wrist identifying me as a dangerous patient.

I promised to be good, and the restraint was removed in a day or two. The orange warning strip, however, remained throughout my residence.

I pleaded that I had broken the rule only because my wife

was not on the premises. After that she stayed in the hospital every night, sleeping on a cot in my room.

Usually she would dash home to have lunch, wash clothes, pick up the mail and feed the dog and five cats. Some nights she went out to dinner with friends, leaving me to survive on hospital food. Having already maligned the hospital unmercifully, I hesitate to add food to my list of its delinquencies. Everyone knows that hospital food is not *haute cuisine*.

I'm sure what I was served was nutritious, with measured amounts of calories and vitamins, but it was entirely without the spices and savories that make food palatable. The hospital is not to be blamed for this deplorable fact. The food was prepared to sustain life, not to enhance it.

Knowing it was good for me did not make it any better. My wife stood by me, virtually force-feeding me, until I had swallowed almost every morsel. The menu was heavy on all the things I don't like—broccoli, spinach, squash, unseasoned meatloaf. Not an egg. Not a strip of bacon. It made me wonder whether life was worth living if one could not enjoy eating.

During my stay at the Huntington, my son Curt sent me a Dave Carpenter cartoon from the Wall Street Journal. It showed a man and woman sitting at the dinner table while their dog lay on the rug, evidently uninterested in scraps. The man is saying, "High fiber. No salt. Low cholesterol. No wonder the dog doesn't beg anymore."

Unfortunately, my wife has conscientiously attempted to duplicate the hospital diet at home. High fiber. No salt. Low cholesterol. No wonder I have no appetite and am down to 150 pounds. I look forward to her breakfast of bacon and eggs, even if the eggs are fake and the bacon is turkey.

She and I went to see my doctor early the other morning and afterward we had breakfast at the Fairway House, a little cafe on Lake in Pasadena. I had the No. 2 breakfast: one egg, two strips of bacon, hash brown potatoes and sourdough toast. It was heavenly.

I will say something good about the Huntington. The nurses are splendid. They were all quick, responsive and good-natured without being saccharine. They giggled at almost everything I said, even though it was often saturnine.

The one who gave me my bath, with a wet towel, was especially prone to laughter, though I don't know what it was about my body that she found so funny. Maybe it was the little tic-tac-toe pattern left on my abdomen by my prostate surgery.

My wife gave the nursing staff two five-pound boxes of chocolates when we left. It must have seemed to them like finding flowers in the desert.

Patients Trying the Patience
of Other Patient Patients

Monday, June 21, 1993

BEFORE I LEAVE my misadventures in Huntington Memorial Hospital behind (which I fervently want to do), I am obliged to correct a few errors I made in trying to recall that unfortunate episode.

In describing a paranoid diatribe I delivered against the hospital and its staff, I noted that Allen Mathies, hospital president, was among my auditors but that he never visited me again. I also said Mathies sent me a single rose in a slender vase.

The amiable Mathies has phoned to remind me that he visited me at least four times and that he sent three roses, not one: a pink, a red and a yellow one. My wife verifies this. It was remarkable of me to remember the one rose. It was pink.

That misbehavior such as mine is not uncommon in hospitals, where patients have usually suffered trauma and are under heavy medication, is evident from the numerous letters I have received relating similar experiences.

"I also made a fool of myself," writes Mrs. John H. Williams. "But people understood and forgave me—even the nurse I slapped."

Even in my most delirious moment, as far as I know, I did not slap a nurse, though some of them must have felt like slapping me.

A woman whose name I will withhold, since she says her husband denies everything, writes that his experience during a recent hospital stay was remarkably like mine. As did my wife, she says, she stood by, maintaining a physical watch over her husband. But one day she took a break from duty, and the hospital called to say that her husband had gone berserk.

"He had one nurse in tears and would not comply with doctor's orders. He had removed IVs and other life-preserving paraphernalia and was now resisting the restraint that would tie him down to the bed."

I sympathize with the guy. I *hated* that.

"In his diatribe against the hospital," she goes on, "he referred to it as an illegal conspiracy and accused the hospital staff of holding him against his will and that it was a scam.

"He promised to report it to the proper authorities. When I tried to persuade him to allow the restraint to be put on him—for his own good—he turned on me and said, 'So you're on their side.' When our daughter intervened, he pointed a finger at her and said, 'You're out of the will.' "

That reminds me of my threat to disinherit my older son unless he got me out of the hospital—which he declined to do.

Pearl Simons, who says she is 74 years old and has all her

marbles, describes her hospital behavior as being much like mine. "And like you, I was out of it. I've been told I was an absolute bitch. I threw my food tray at a nurse. They moved my roommate out in the middle of the night."

When it came time to release her, Mrs. Simons refused to sign the papers. She couldn't believe she had been in the hospital that long.

During his nine weeks in Arcadia Methodist Hospital, writes Charles Davis Smith, he also pulled tubes and catheters from his body and demanded paper on which he scribbled "Call 911.... Don't tell nurse.... Call police...." His demands were no more availing than mine.

Of his recent experience, Roy Churchill writes, "Before the hospital released me, I had terrorized the entire staff. Like you, I was convinced I was being held prisoner.

"My final act of defiance was pulling out all tubes, trying to pull out the catheter, then walking stark naked down the hall."

I don't remember if I ever walked stark naked down the hall. The question is academic anyway. Those hospital gowns must be worn open down the back and are very hard to tie, so that one's fundaments are usually in full view. The first thing you surrender in a hospital is privacy.

Robert F. Pace tells a now-familiar story. Like me, he was dependent on the accounts of witnesses for clues to his behavior during three weeks in an East Coast hospital. "I was appalled at what my wife and nieces told me about my 'hazy' days and nights.

"I broke restraints, used vile language on those taking care of me, threatened to sue, even shoot them. A priest was called in some three times."

I think I did everything these patients confess to except threaten to shoot my tormentors. That restraint, I suspect, was only because I did not have access to a gun.

Being a man of no religion, I was not ministered to by a priest. I think the appearance of a priest at my bedside would have killed me.

But it's an ill wind that blows no good. I now have a handicapped parking permit.

Not a Shingle Moment
Without a Symptom

Monday, July 19, 1993

W H E N   I   L I S T E D our recent household breakdowns the other day, I limited it for some reason to mechanical calamities, not personal.

I don't know why I made this distinction, but perhaps it was because of some eerie suspicion that forces beyond the pale were involved, and perhaps I didn't want to annoy them.

When you know that some evil entity has the power to break a pipe or make a faucet stick, you are inclined to treat it with respect, if not with awe.

Are the gods who control broken light bulbs more important than those who control broken kneecaps?

I was also guilty of some slipshod reporting, or perhaps overdramatizing when I referred to my heart attack as disastrous. It seemed so at the time, but a few weeks later, when I got a second attack, the first one seemed almost benign by comparison.

My first attack evidently was a myocardial infarction. It occurred after prostate surgery at Huntington Memorial Hospital. It was a staggering blow. I called it devastating.

After I had generated a considerable amount of sympathy for this tale, the paramedics took me at 4 o'clock one morning to Los Angeles County USC Medical Center. Nine years previously, the paramedics had taken me to the same emergency room. My heart had stopped in emergency, and a young nurse had started it again with a shock and saved my life.

This time I suffered what was called congestive heart failure. After my condition had been stabilized, they moved me back to Huntington to be with my doctors. The doctors discovered that somewhere along the line I had also suffered a stroke. The stroke was truly devastating.

My previous accounts of my illness have identified only those symptoms that were evident after the post-prostate heart attack. Those suffered in the later stroke, whenever that was, were much worse. I cannot walk.

This is a fate much worse than any I ever imagined for myself. I haven't been bad enough to deserve that, have I? There are no moral implications in broken light bulbs and leaky faucets, but when you start being punished for your general conduct, it makes you wonder. I am certainly no more guilty of bad manners than Job was. I've always thought that Job made a pretty good case for himself. If it comes down to my credentials against his, I think my case would stand up in court.

The odd thing is that I have had two shots at it. In the first one, my punishment was comparatively mild, though we see now that that judgment was relative. It didn't seem so mild when I first began limping through Sycamore Grove on my daily walk with my wife. Also I felt quite justified when I applied for and received my handicapped parking permit. It has since been upgraded in validity.

At the time, to a man who had usually been sound of body, that being a given of life, I was seriously downgraded by the accident. Ever since then I have been wishing I could exchange the later attack for the first one. Talk about being unfair.

Even more strange than these apparent accidents are their number and sequence. No sooner had the first attack left me crippled than I was troubled by abdominal pains whose source I didn't know. They finally became unbearable and I went to the doctor. He said, "You have diverticulitis."

He prescribed an antibiotic and promised that the pain would be gone in three days. In three days the pain was worse. He told me to come in. Meanwhile I had developed some itchy sores in the small of my back. I assumed they were bites. But they were growing larger and more painful.

The doctor had me take my T-shirt off. He said, "You don't have diverticulitis. You have shingles." I was shocked. What a strange disease for a grown man to get. It was a virus held over from chicken pox and released when immunity was low. The doctor prescribed a pain killer and a specific. The pain continued for several days as the childhood disease attacked me in my old age.

I do not have appointments with my various doctors, but they show up on the scene from time to time in the hospital. One does not have old-fashioned talks as in the past. Generally I encounter one of them and try to zero in with a few pertinent questions before he gets away. One's most meaningful dialogues with one's doctor are usually conducted in this manner.

The other day I saw one of my doctors standing in my hospital room. He said hello and asked the usual inconsequential questions. He was Dr. Anchel Furman, an internist. I had talked to him briefly on several occasions. He was adept at the brief quizzical remark. I asked him, "Doctor, what misfortune will I suffer next?"

"No more," he said. "God is tired."

Photographs

Jack at Work

Jack at his desk at the Daily News, circa 1948

EARLY IN OUR MARRIAGE *of 56 years it dawned on me that Jack had a mistress and I had a life-long rival: the newspaper business. This was a triangle I decided I could live with. When newspapermen gathered and talked shop, their conversation was not limited, as it is in so many other professions. They talked about the whole world, the people in it, and the strange and silly and wonderful and terrible things they do to and for each other. The prospect of sharing Jack with this powerful rival was intimidating, but exhilarating, and I never (or almost never) begrudged the fact that she usually came first in his consideration.* —Denny

Reporting a story on Los Angeles Athletic Club, late 1960s

Jack (third from left) after hours at a newsman's saloon, mid-1950s

"We were a disreputable lot, but we kept the people informed, at least about the lower reaches of society. Stanley Walker had defined news as 'wine, women and wampum,' and we covered it."

Jack at Home

Curt, Denny, Jack and Doug, late 1970s

DAD WAS ALWAYS *acutely aware that he could embarrass us.
That's why for many years he would identify us in his columns
without using our names. Instead, he referred to his wife,
his older or younger son, his Italian or French daughter-in-law
and his oldest or youngest grandson or granddaughter.
He only changed this practice when Curtis Kelly, the editor
of God and Mr. Gomez, one of his books, asked him
if his wife had a name other than "my wife." After that
we had names. Still, he wrote about us with affection and made
himself the butt of his jokes, not those of us who had no way
to defend ourselves.* —Curt

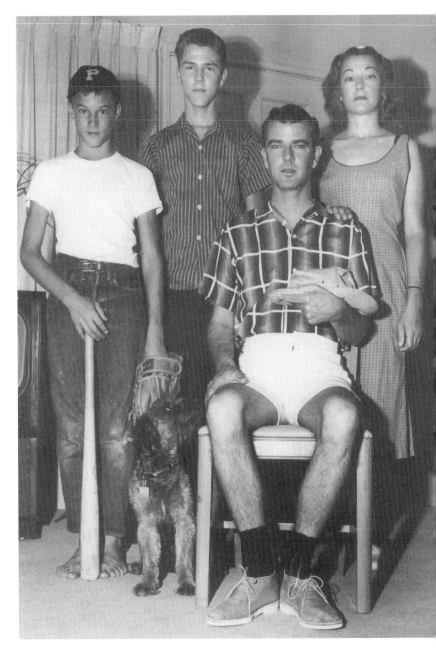

Doug, Curt, Jack and Denny—and faithful canine Gene Biscailuz—circa 1958

Brother Harry, sister Permelia and mother Anna.
Whittier, California, Easter Sunday, circa 1960

'In my later years my life has become dominated by women. It's a fate that seems to overtake many men, but somehow I escaped in childhood. Neither my mother nor my older sister had much influence over me."

Jack and Denny with Alison, Casey and Trevor, 1985

"Sometimes I doubt that the Creator's plan is infallible, but He certainly was right in arranging for children to be given to young adults, and not to their elders."

"Never having had a daughter, I am especially fascinated by my two granddaughters, though I wouldn't say that they yet hold me in mindless esteem or regard me as a fountain of wisdom."

Grandpa Smith with Adriana, June, 1988

"**H**e was going to a new world. He was a soldier, not a boot....We knew, as the Army says, that he was going to be all that he can be."

Jackie, Jack and Doug attend Chris's graduation from U.S. Army basic training, Fort Benning, Georgia, February, 1992

The Smith clan at Alison's graduation from Brentwood School, June 1995.
Gail is on the right

'Thus I, the paterfamilias, am surrounded and supported by exemplary grandchildren. The word 'family' never seems to be used in a positive sense anymore, but I would say we are a functional one."

Jack and Denny celebrate the 50th anniversary of their June 17, 1939, marriage

"My wife says her kitchen range is 50 years old. I point out that it still works, but she says that's beside the point. Well, our marriage is more than 50 years old. And it still works. Doesn't it?"

Jack at Large

READERS OFTEN WONDERED *if we spent our lives
bent over in stitches because our father was such a funny man.
The truth is that we did get some belly laughs out of his early
aches and pains and we were amused by his wry anecdotes
when he spoke in public. But when we genuinely reflect on this
question, we all agree that the "real" Jack Smith was not funny.
The man we knew was intense, mentally energetic, occasionally
caustic or sarcastic, and always at least partially engaged in writing
his next column. That was the journalist. The father was sensitive,
hopeful and, like all parents, not quite sure how to talk
to his children. I think he harbored regrets about the harshness
of his youth and had a real desire to become more like
the suave and witty public persona he had created.
And, over the years, he gradually became that man.* —Doug

One of Jack's many
appearances before
the Press Club

Iwo Jima Island, February, 1945, in early days of U.S. Marine invasion, researching a name for his first born

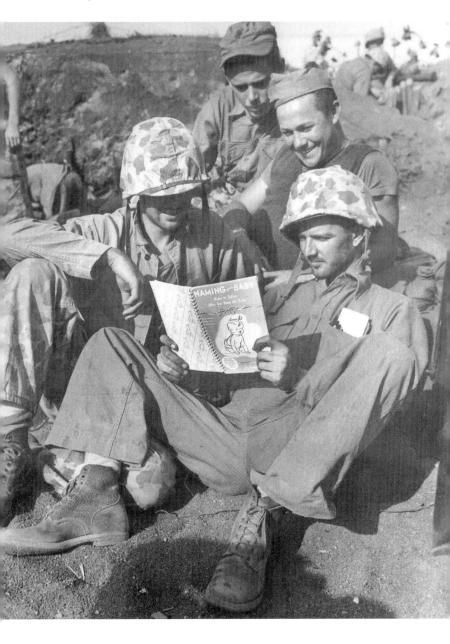

Ever in tune with the times, Jack dresses for the Beatles' first U.S. tour

"I gave Gomez a check for $100, and we sealed the bargain with a sho of tequila. In Baja, any deal that is sealed with tequila is binding."

Jack helps the late Mr. Gomez construct the Baja getaway.
Early 1970s, Puerto Santo Tomas

Hospital Rehab a Boot Camp
With Cocktails

Monday, July 26, 1993

I AM NOW in residence at the Huntington Memorial Hospital rehabilitation wing. It is something like a Riviera hotel with roses and geraniums outside our window, sunflowers in our room and a cool ocean breeze. We even have room service, though there the similarity ends.

In some respects it reminds me of boot camp. The wing's function is to rehabilitate patients who have been crippled by strokes and other neurological accidents. The instructors are mostly voluptuous young women, cheerful but rather fierce in their dedication to their work.

In boot camp I never had a drill instructor land on me the way these women do. "Pick that foot up! Move it! Stand up straight!" They don't seem to realize they are talking to a tired, old man who has been severely treated by the gods. On the other hand I never had a drill instructor who gave me a bath, which one of my nurses did. He would have been drummed out of the corps.

Usually it is one on one, with one instructor haranguing the patient. I dread these sessions, though one could hardly ask to spend half an hour with a more buoyant young woman. Sometimes they work with groups. The other day, a young male instructor got a group of us into a volleyball game with a pink balloon. Despite my infirmities, I was rather the star. My old sense of timing was intact.

However, nothing else was. My nervous system is awry. My DI says I will soon be walking, but I do not believe her. The height seems too great to surmount.

Meanwhile, I am trying. We shall see.

There is also a speech therapy phase of the training. I would have thought that my speech was unaffected since my conversation seems to remain uninhibited, if generally pessimistic.

The tests they give you, however, are tricky. Some are true or false and extremely easy. For example: Abraham Lincoln was the first President of the United States. Another was trickier: In the United States anyone can get a license to drive a car. Well, that's easy enough, isn't it? Everyone is permitted to take the test, and if you can pass it you get a license. On the other hand, what if you're blind? I answered yes, which will probably go down on my record as a blot.

The other day in a word test, they gave me three words—*apple, mountain, truth*—and told me to remember them; they would ask me for them later. When we finished the session, they thanked me and said goodbye. I said, "What about *apple, mountain* and *truth*?" They looked embarrassed. One said to the other, "He wins. You get a demerit."

Today I was given four words to remember and asked later to repeat them. I could remember only two. The therapist gave me hints about the other two and I finally remembered that they were *piano* and *green*. However, I have now forgotten the first two.

I confessed to the young women that while my tests may not show it, I am having trouble with my short-term memory. I cannot remember words that I have recently acquired, particularly those associated with my various diseases.

When my doctor diagnosed one of them as diverticulitis, the word refused to become part of my vocabulary until he reversed himself and decided I didn't have it. The same thing happened with shingles, a childhood disease that I contracted recently. To this day I cannot remember the word and knew it only because I asked my wife.

There have been occasional moments of conviviality, despite the stringent hospital rules. The other night we had a cocktail party in our room, which I suspect was an unprecedented event. Our internist, Dr. Andrew Muller, had given me permission to have one vodka tonic a night, showing his liberal streak. So my wife had brought a bottle of vodka, some tonic water, limes and tall glasses to my room. That evening three young relatives came by and I asked them if they'd like a vodka tonic. All three agreed enthusiastically. My wife poured. It was a delightful interlude, the more so because of a sense of conspiracy and a defiance of the rules. None of our fellow residents believe the story.

Room service is excellent, if somewhat overzealous. We have buzzers that we push to call the nurses. They quickly bring pills or whatever comfort you need. The other night I asked my nurse to give me an enema. I had been having trouble with my bowels and was in severe pain.

She got my doctor's permission and gave me an enema with great dispatch. I was relieved of my distress and spent a comfortable evening. She is a jewel.

What hotel on the Riviera would give you room service like that?

Worn Out Wife
Runs Out of Gas...Literally

Monday, August 9, 1993

WE CHECKED OUT of Huntington Memorial Hospital the other day after 32 days of uncomfortable residence in the medical intensive care unit, the progressive care unit and the rehabilitation wing. My physical therapists worked hard on me; they say I can walk, but I point out that it is only for a short distance and very precariously. In time, they say, if I keep to a regimen of exercises, I will eventually walk like a man.

My wife stayed with me the whole time, though she was a squatter. She slept in my room on a cot, but when meals were served to me she didn't get any. Sometimes she stole my leftovers; sometimes she ate in the hospital cafeteria; sometimes she had lunch at home when she went back to do the laundry and feed the dog and the cats.

It could not have been easy for her. She had to fetch all my props—my cough drops, my urinal, my nose spray, my TV Guide, my water, my paper, my book, my glasses and numerous other articles that were always being misplaced beyond my reach.

Every night she was awakened at least four times by nurses who came to take my blood, give me pills or give me an insulin shot. Every time I went to the bathroom either she or a nurse had to go with me. The first thing you surrender when you enter a hospital is privacy.

In her effort to keep up my morale, she wrote an inspirational motto each morning on the room's blackboard. Some were literary, some were nursery level. They ranged from Goethe's last words (according to reader Joseph D. Alstater), *Lasset Licht herein*—"Let light come in" to "Let a little sunshine in."

She also used *Yhee or*, which is Hebrew for "Let there be light," and which happens to be my personalized license plate.

I liked "Let a little sunshine in" because it demonstrated the folly of that alleged rule of grammar that one must not end a sentence with a preposition. How would you say it? "Let in a little sunshine"?

The first day, as I remember, she used the Latin phrase, *carpe diem*, which means "Seize the day." Plainly that meant one should take each day and use it to the fullest—not an easy thing to do in a hospital. Another was *Litera scripta manet*— "The written word remains"—from Horace.

My favorite, though, was a Chinese proverb I poached from a copy of Bartlett's "Familiar Quotations" my wife brought from home. "Keep a green tree in your heart and perhaps the singing bird will come."

I wish she had used one of mine. "Keep your gas tank full of gas and you won't run out." My wife tends to run on a low tank, arguing that she is too busy to stop at a station. My argument that excuses won't fill a tank is unavailing. On the evening before our departure she was supposed to bring my new wheelchair to the hospital for a checkout. She was supposed to be there by 6 p.m. She loaded the chair in her car and tried to start it. No luck. Soon half a dozen neighbors were poking at the car, trying to fix it. They decided it was out of gas. They replenished it with pots and pans of gas from other sources.

Then the starter wouldn't work. Evidently one of the men had broken it by using too much force. Eventually a neighbor put the wheelchair in his car and drove her to the hospital. She was only half an hour late. Meanwhile, I sat in excruciating anxiety, feeling quite helpless, which I was.

My wife argues that by filling my car when it's only half empty, I have to go to a gas station twice as often as she does. What folly that notion is.

We left without fanfare, except for some emotional good-bys to our nurses. They had been wonderful.

Oddly, the thing I appreciated most about being home was the quiet. Hospitals are full of nerve-racking sounds. Bells ringing. Beds and other wheeled things being rolled down hallways. The screams of patients. A man in the room next to ours kept yelling "Mom!" The chattering of patients and their families in nearby rooms. The yammering of television.

There is not much good to say about a hospital stay. But there were one or two things that weren't entirely disagreeable. I didn't mind the young woman who gave me a shower every other day. She also offered to shave me, but some male things are too intimate to share.

I do not expect the peace and quiet to last long at home. My wife is about to remodel again. She wants to do her bathroom and the kitchen over. She says her kitchen range is 50 years old.

I point out that it still works, but she says that's beside the point. Well, our marriage is more than 50 years old. And it still works. Doesn't it?

Playboy a Rookie
Next to Women's Magazines

Monday, June 27, 1994

A U.S. DISTRICT COURT ruling has solved a problem for me—a problem that was growing more acute with each passing month.

The problem: What to do with my back issues of Playboy magazine. I must have 60 of them stacked behind doors in a living room cabinet.

You might wonder why I save them. It is not to satisfy my prurient interest, although that may be a minor factor. Actually, the magazine has an intrinsic value that is not diminished by time. For one thing, the female figure has not changed much over the millennia. She is still as alluring as Eve.

More pertinent, old Playboys have a monetary value that does not diminish with age. Several years ago I gave a stack to the PTA for a sale it was holding at Carlin G. Smith playground on Mt. Washington. They discreetly placed them under the table and sold every one at $2.50 a copy.

More recently, I've given several copies to my old friend Romulo Gomez when he's in town from Baja. He says they don't have any Playboys in Mexico.

Now, thanks to the decision by U.S. District Judge Stephen V. Wilson voiding a county ruling that firemen could not keep or read Playboy in firehouses, I feel free to give my old copies to firemen.

This county rule evidently was prompted by a fear that reading the magazine and looking at its color spreads of nude women would incite firemen to acts of sexual harassment. The judge ruled that this restraint was a violation of the constitutional amendment guaranteeing free speech.

If Playboy is to be banned for creating a highly charged sexual atmosphere, what about women's magazines? They are far worse.

While waiting for my manicurist the other day, I was glancing at a pile of magazines on her table and my eye was caught by a title on the cover of the Ladies Home Journal: "Sexual Sins: What you shouldn't do in bed." My curiosity aroused, I read the article but didn't learn anything I didn't already know.

Later that day, while waiting in Vons while my wife shopped, I glanced at the women's magazines in a rack. Mademoiselle featured an article called "How to Make Sex Better—Really, *Really* Better." It also featured an article called "A Great Butt: Exercises That Do It." Glamour advertised "Hate Your Contraceptive? Women Rate a New Method."

Complete Woman featured an article on "Men and Sex:

Secrets Every Woman (You!) Must Know."

Woman's Own advertised "Men and Sex: At Last! Real Men Tell 'What Makes a Woman Good in Bed.'" That same issue also features "Marital Secrets: Which to Confess and When to Keep Your Mouth Shut."

The old respectable Redbook has an article titled "Orgasm School: 15 Lessons You'll Love to Learn."

While I was sitting at the deli counter drinking a Coke, a man sitting beside me got up to leave and shoved aside a magazine he had been reading. Evidently he had taken it from the rack and not paid for it. It was VW Trends, a magazine for Volkswagen aficionados. I figured it probably wouldn't have any sexy pictures in it.

But it happened to be the magazine's annual Super Swimsuit Spectacular. There were eight pages of full-color pictures of well endowed young women in the skimpiest of bikinis. All were either sitting in or leaning against Volkswagens. I was beginning to feel that there was no escape from sex (there isn't, really).

Meanwhile, my new Playboy has come. It features nine pages of color photographs of Patti Davis, the rebel daughter of Ronald and Nancy Reagan. She is absolutely starkers. The only thing this revealing spread proves is that Patti had good genes.

It also contains a thought-piece on gun control by Robert Scheer, a regular columnist, and an enlightening article on prostate cancer. I think that would be of more value to a male firefighter than what not to say in bed.

I wonder whether a male firefighter would be more likely to harass a female firefighter after seeing a picture of Patti Davis in the nude or reading an article on "How to Make Sex Better—Really, *Really* Better." I also wonder whether an article on prostate cancer or a think-piece on gun control is as likely to titillate a male firefighter into harassing one of his colleagues than 15 lessons on orgasm.

This controversy gives me an idea for a random act of senseless kindness, an activity in which my readers seem to feel I have been delinquent.

I would be happy to deliver a few back issues of Playboy to any fire station whose firefighters ask for them.

After all, a male firefighter's job is to rush into the streets when he hears the alarm, and risk his life to save the lives of others. What would be more likely to inspire him to this act of bravery than pictures of live young women?

Meanwhile, maybe the county should consider banning *women's* magazines from fire stations.

Facing the Naked Truth About His Caregiver

Monday, August 16, 1993

ONCE A WEEK at the Huntington Hospital rehabilitation center a committee of doctors, nurses and therapists meets to review patients' progress and decide their fate.

The committee ruled that I was fit to be dismissed from the hospital on a certain Saturday but that I was not "independent." That meant that I would need constant help to get around and do what I had to do.

For eight weeks my wife had been taking care of me. But all her vacation time was used up and she had to get back to work. She is administrative director of the Southern California Counseling Center. Not only do they need her there, but she loves her work and missed it.

I insisted that she go back to work. Taking care of me was

not easy. She had begun forgetting things or getting things wrong. She is usually so efficient and reliable that I realized she needed some relief. She even had to go to the bathroom with me to make sure I didn't lose my balance and take a tumble in my walker. A broken hip would have been the last straw.

I am supposed to call her before I get up to go anywhere. One of the hardest things to recover after a stroke, I found out, is one's sense of balance. I tend to fall to the right.

My daughter-in-law Jackie had bought me a silver bell to use in calling my wife, but our house is large and she did not always hear it. So my other daughter-in-law, Gail, brought me a coach's whistle, which does the job, but whose shrill summons must be nerve-racking to the poor wretch for whom it is intended.

All these problems concerned us when we realized we would have to hire someone to take my wife's place. Who could possibly fill that bill? It would have to be someone who was physically strong, temperamentally tough and monumentally patient. I am not the easiest person to take care of, especially now that I am physically limited.

We discussed it. I said one thing was certain. It would have to be a woman. She pointed out that the job would require physical strength, if just for getting my wheelchair in and out of the car. I pointed out that the suggestion that a woman wasn't strong enough was sexist, which she isn't.

"Speaking of being sexist," she said, and she reminded me of the time I wanted to hire an Occidental College woman undergraduate to work in my office with me and help with my files and books.

"Don't forget," she said. "Under equal rights you can't insist on a woman. You have to take whoever is best qualified."

I pointed out that I have always preferred the company of women, and that I would not be temperamentally suited to working in close confinement with a man. I like men. I like their company. But I would not want to be dependent on one for intimate services.

My wife called a couple of agencies that handle such help and the manager of one said she had just the woman. She recently spent four years taking care of a man and his wife who were invalids. The man was in a wheelchair. The woman finally died and the man went to live with relatives.

She sounded all right and she agreed to visit us at our house for an interview. One thing she had to be able to do, of course, was drive, because she had to shuttle me to my therapy sessions, to the doctor and perhaps to lunch.

She arrived at our house right on time, though she had taken the back way, the hard way, up the hill. People have been lost for days finding our house.

"I know you can drive," I said, "or you wouldn't be here."

She said she drove a little Dodge Colt but it was big enough for a wheelchair and for me.

Her name is Donnie Ware. I liked the look of her. She is 5 feet 10, and strong. She looks like she could handle anything, including me. She said her son Nathan was 6 feet 8, a Lynwood High basketball star and college prospect.

I decided she would do, but there was one contingency I hadn't covered. I had been taking a shower every other day, an enterprise so potentially dangerous that my wife had to stand by me throughout.

My wife said she could give me the shower in the evening, after dinner. But I said I would rather have it in the late afternoon.

"Then Donnie will have to give it to you," she said.

"There's one thing I have to ask you," I said to Donnie. "Would it bother you to see me naked?"

"No, not at all," she said. Somehow I was disappointed.

Toasting His Past Cars
With a Lemon Twist

Monday, September 6, 1993

B E I N G   U N A B L E , for the time being at least, to drive, I feel dispossessed. A man who can't drive in Los Angeles is not truly an independent or functioning citizen.

It's not that my car has been idle. Both my sons have borrowed it when theirs were in the shop. (My younger son, Doug, has a sickly old Porsche that seems to need periodic and prolonged attention.)

I am glad to see my car used, but sometimes I long to be behind the wheel for a run over the freeways. No man ever forgets a car he has owned. I have owned many—mostly lemons. Most of them I purchased used, and then used them until they dropped dead. As a boy I never tinkered with engines, and never learned how to take care of a car.

My first car was a used 1929 Ford roadster bought for me by my father while I was a senior in high school. I remember driving it down the street past the school, hoping girls would run out crying for a ride. Nothing like that happened. It was a lemon as a girl catcher and as a car. It was 5 years old and had evidently been grievously misused. Its rings were gone. I had to put a quart of oil in it every 25 miles.

My next car was the best car I ever had. As I remember, it was a 1922 Model T Ford. It was black, like most Fords of that vintage, and looked like a sedan chair.

I think I paid $20 for it on Figueroa Street when I was in the Civilian Conservation Corps. That would have been about 1935. I was assistant editor of the March Field Courier, a newspaper for

30 Southern California CCC camps. I cut the logo out of our paper, COURIER, pasted it on my windshield and drove that Model T all over the Southland hills, visiting camps for news.

After I left the CCC, I had the vainglorious idea of driving the old Ford down the Baja peninsula all the way to La Paz over a road that was then virtually an untracked wilderness. I set out one day on that adventure, heading for San Bernardino to pick up an equally foolhardy friend, but the car died on the road, evidently from old age. I sold it to a junk man in San Bernardino for $4.

My next car was not nearly as good a car, but it is memorable because it was the car in which I courted my wife-to-be. I don't know how it's done today, but most courtships in those days were carried out in the front seats of cars. It was a 1933 Ford V-8 and it, too, died on the road, probably from neglect, while my wife and I were driving from Bakersfield to Fresno for a funeral.

When I got out of the Marine Corps after the war and went to work for the San Diego Journal, my mother bought me a 1941 Packard sedan, one of the last made before the wartime conversion of auto plants into armament factories. It was black and sleek, the classiest car I ever owned, but I drove it into the ground and sold it to a man I met in a bar for $600. Without wheels, I was obliged to ride the Red Car to work for months.

My first new car was a British Anglia that I bought in about 1950. It was a midget, with cylinders the size of teacups. I don't remember what happened to it, but it couldn't have been good.

My favorite car of all, aside from that 1922 Ford, was a brand new Dodge convertible, white with black leather upholstery. I never felt so right in a car as I did when I drove that baby over the Pasadena Freeway with the top down. I put 120,000 miles on that Dodge, but it finally died one day after a hose broke and it overheated. I gave it to our housecleaner for her son, who put a truck engine in it and probably drove it for years.

I next bought a Chevrolet Luv pickup which we did drive to La Paz. I traded the Luv for a Nova sedan. Red, brand new. It wasn't sporty enough for me, after the convertible, so I gave it to my wife, who had already gone through a red Mustang and a Cougar with a houndstooth top.

Today we both drive Japanese cars, to the annoyance of some critics who think we should have bought American. Hers is a 9-year-old Maxima, which she loves, though I think it's a lemon; mine is a 1991 Honda Civic. My Civic isn't much for picking up girls, but neither am I anymore.

Pedicure His Most Elevating Feat Ever

Monday, November 8, 1993

I T I S N E V E R too late for one to set out on new adventures.

The other day, for example, I had my first pedicure. A few times in my life I have had manicures, but never a pedicure.

The need arose because I find it hard to cut my toenails. For one thing, diabetics are warned not to cut their own toenails for fear of inflicting a wound that could lead to blood poisoning and the loss of a leg. That made it seem hardly worth the risk.

For another, my right leg is rather unmanageable because of my stroke, and I find it hard to bring my foot up high enough to work on the nails. Besides, my toenails are hard and tough, about the consistency, I would imagine, of a rhinoceros horn.

My wife offered to trim them for me, but she was unable to

cut through them with my fingernail scissors. "Why don't you go get a pedicure?" she suggested.

I had heard of pedicures, of course, but I had supposed that only women got them. Women often paint and display their toenails in public, and it was only natural that they would want them to look trim. Besides, I supposed, pedicures were a function of the beauty shop, not the barber shop. I couldn't imagine a man sitting in a barber chair and reading the sports section while having his toenails trimmed. Ridiculous.

"Where do I get a pedicure?" I asked my wife.

"A beauty shop, I suppose," she said.

"Have you ever had one?"

"No, but I probably ought to."

I had been to a beauty shop only once before in my life. I came out with a permanent wave. As luck would have it, I had to go into the hospital before the wave grew out, and I was sorely embarrassed.

I didn't even know where a beauty shop was. Donnie Ware, the woman who drives me about, said she had seen one down the hill in the little mall at Avenue 43 and Figueroa Street. She said a sign in the window advertised pedicures for both men and women. (She notices things.)

It sounded like my kind of place. We drove down to the Packard Grill for lunch, but I stopped in at Lilly's Beauty Salon. I asked if I could make an appointment for a pedicure at 2 o'clock and was told that the woman who did pedicures was out but would be back by 2. We had lunch and went back to the beauty salon.

The pedicurist was there. She was very businesslike about the pedicure. She told me to sit down and take my shoes and socks off—a procedure she helped me with—then had me put my bare feet in a small plastic tub of hot, soapy water.

She began preparing my feet, scrubbing them with a brush,

applying mysterious oils and unguents, and drying them with a towel.

She used a large steel clipper to cut the nails. Snip. Snip. It obviously took strong, practiced hands. I thought it must be demeaning to wash someone else's feet, but then I remembered that Jesus had done it, so it must be all right.

She worked fast. Now and then she made a remark and giggled. I couldn't always understand her remarks, but the giggles were reassuring. She was happy in her work. When she finished cutting the nails, she polished them with some soothing liquid on a cotton ball, then oiled and massaged my feet and calves. It was absolutely sybaritic. For a moment I floated off in a dream.

Then she dried my feet and went to work on my hands. The bill was $14—$9 for the pedicure and $5 for the manicure. I felt so euphoric I tipped her $5 and promised to be back in a month or less.

She gave me her card. "Nails by Nancy."

My mood remained elevated throughout the evening. When my wife got home from work, I took off my shoes and socks and showed her my toenails. She couldn't believe it. "How did she manage to cut those things?"

I felt so sociable I wanted to go out in society and show my toenails. I called my French daughter-in-law and invited her out to dinner. (Her husband was working late and couldn't come.) We ate at Roxxi. I wanted to take my shoes off and show her my toenails, but I realized that a restaurant was hardly the place for such an exhibition.

"I got a pedicure today," I told her over the wine. "Mr. Smith!" she exclaimed. "You didn't!" She acted as if I had exposed a new and fascinating side of my character.

I wondered how many other gratifying experiences I haven't yet dared to have in life.

CHAPTER 12

Trying (Hard) to Keep Upright

Best-Dressed Omission
Suits Him Just Fine

Monday April 20, 1992

M Y   R E C E N T   L A M E N T   about being overlooked again as
one of America's 10 best-dressed men has brought an enlightening letter from actor Eddie Albert.

Albert's story of his own selection bears out my suspicion
that the Tailors Council of America, which picks the 10
best, is guided more by a candidate's celebrity than by his
taste in clothes.

I have always explained my own exclusion, year after year,
by my naive assumption that the council employed scouts to
roam the country, looking for well-dressed men, and that I was
never chosen because a scout apprehended me on a day that I
was wearing something my wife bought me by mail order.

Albert's story bears out my underlying suspicion that the
council is more interested in who you are than how you look.
For example, the basketball star Michael Jordan was among last
year's selectees, but how many of us have ever seen him in
anything but his basketball togs?

It is true, however, that he is impeccably attired for his
sport. I am reminded of the World War II story of the British
subaltern and the Wren who were caught frolicking in the
nude in the Raffles Hotel. Court-martialed for being out of
uniform, they were acquitted on the grounds that they were
properly attired for the activity in which they were engaged.

"A few years back," Albert writes, "I received a phone call
from New York, from a person who represented the National
Tailors and who told me that I had been voted Best Dressed

Actor of the Year.

"I thanked him but protested that there must be an error, that he wanted Eddie Arnold or Eddie Murphy. He protested, no—they wanted me (with only three suits, none less than 10 years old) and that they would give me a beautiful plaque, and a thrilling gathering, a luncheon at the Waldorf in the big ballroom on March-the-whatever and much publicity, and said it was a great honor. I said I was heartsick, but on that date, I was getting married, or confirmed, or de-wormed, I forget which, and that I would be unable to be in New York on that date, and I would be so grateful if they would put the beautiful plaque in the mail.

" 'Oh, no,' he said. 'To receive the plaque you would have to show up here in New York, personally, at the luncheon.' I replied that in that case I would have to decline the honor, that the date made it impossible for me.

"He expressed considerable distress and was sorry it couldn't work out. Then he thought a moment, and said, 'Mr. Albert, could you suggest anyone else?' "

It occurs to me that Albert might very well have suggested me. I have met Albert several times in recent years at the home of his neighbor, Mary Anita Loos, in Pacific Palisades. I don't remember how Albert was dressed, but I believe I always dressed in casual elegance for Mary Anita's parties, and it wouldn't surprise me that I caught his eye. But he obviously did not recommend me, since I was never selected.

I met Albert again several years later at a big dinner in the Beverly Hilton. Some big Jewish charitable organization was giving awards to several Southlanders for their contributions to the community, and I was among them. Albert was master of ceremonies. Since we both wore tuxedos, it was not an occasion for comparing our outfits, the tuxedo leaving its wearer little room for individual expression.

I remember that evening for a remark of mine that Albert unwittingly set up. The man he introduced just before me was in his 80s, and Albert said, "Better an old eagle than a young sparrow, eh?"

Then he introduced me.

I stepped up to the microphone and said, "Ladies and gentlemen, you're looking at an old sparrow."

I'd rather have said that than be selected as one of the 10 best-dressed.

His Latest Challenge
With Cane vs. Able

Monday, November 21, 1994

O N E   T H I N G a columnist ought to have is balance.

I think I have had pretty good balance over the 30 years or so I have been writing this column.

But I seem to have lost it, politically, if I ever had it. In the recent election, I voted on the losing side in all the big races. Of course, I may have been right.

More grievous is the loss of my sense of physical balance. I no longer have the automatic balancing skill that most of us acquire before the age of 2. I cannot walk safely without a cane or my wife's arm—and even with those two props, my walking is precarious.

I am prone to falling, and a fall can be disastrous. One can break an arm or a leg or even a hip. I have chipped an ankle, bruised both my elbows and a shoulder, and, as I have already said, broken my left wrist.

Even with my cane, which I do not use very skillfully, walking is dangerous. I was coming out of the bathroom into the hall when I lost my balance and fell. My wife was in the hall but did not become aware of my predicament in time to save me. I did the usual flinging out of arms and crashed to the floor.

She went to her knees, wailing, and gathered me up in her arms, but the damage was done. A broken radius.

A broken wrist is more disabling than I had imagined. Not only does one lose the skills ordinarily performed by the wrist, such as typing and driving a wheelchair, but it becomes impossible to fold a newspaper back to an inside page.

More devastating is the loss of balance a free swinging left arm provides. The added weight of the Fiberglas cast deprives one of this automatic skill.

My wife rented a wheelchair and hired a woman to help me. But I do not call on her as often as I should. After all, I have a sense of adventure and think I can make it by myself. The result is too many close calls.

Some of the most ordinary human pastimes become perilous. The other evening my wife and I went out for a reception at Chasen's. The room was overcrowded with guests, including celebrities such as Kirk Douglas, Charlton Heston, Hal Linden, Mariette Hartley, Roddy McDowall and Gordon Davidson, artistic director of Center Theatre Group. It was a celebration of the reopening of the remodeled Ahmanson Theatre.

A cocktail party is especially treacherous for a man with no balance. One is liable to be knocked over by a guest—even by a petite woman—and sent sprawling.

I had asked a waitress to get me a chair and she did, a small wooden one, placing it at the edge of the crowd. I was sitting on it drinking a vodka tonic, when I lost my balance and began to slide off. My wife had warned me not to spill the drink and I remember thrusting my right arm out in an effort to save it.

I was already off the chair and slipping toward the floor when I was grabbed by a strong arm that righted me and lifted me to my feet. My savior was none other than that heroic figure of the screen—Kirk Douglas.

Of course, I can't always count on such a practiced hero as Douglas to rescue me, but I wonder if I couldn't get him to retype these essays for me.

Using the touch system is hopeless. The result reads like this: *Tqui kb roddwwn fox jumped over thaae lazy dog;s bsack.*

So I am reduced to the tortuous pick-and-peck system.

It is heartbreaking to watch athletes or dancers on television. When I see Joe Montana roll out of the pocket and throw for a touchdown or watch Ginger Rogers and Fred Astaire in one of their dazzling routines, I feel like a clod.

All my life it has been my ambition to tap-dance. Several years ago, Douglas and Burt Lancaster did a little soft shoe together at the Academy Awards. It was lovely—those two big men tapping about so lightly and so gracefully.

I was so pleased that I wrote a paragraph about their dance and was delighted to receive a note of thanks from Lancaster.

Once I went so far as to enroll in a tap-dancing class in the Valley, but I attended only one session. Of course there are many other things I wish I had taken time to learn, but I had tap-dancing within my grasp and let it get away.

If there is a moral in this sorry tale, it is that one ought to take the time to do what one yearns to do. And don't break a wrist.

He's Fallen Down
and Can't Reach His Alarm

Monday, November 28, 1994

T H E R E   W A S quite a commotion at our house the other day.

Trying to reach something on the end table beside my bed, I slid off and bounced on the floor, knocking over a soup bowl, a glass of water and a plate of lunch leftovers.

Because of my instability I am supposed to wear an alarm cord around my neck. It has buttons for 911, police, fire department, a neighbor and nearby relatives. However, I often neglect to put it on when my wife leaves me alone. I'm afraid I will set it off accidentally.

One day a few weeks ago, I evidently pushed some of the buttons by accident just before my wife and I left the house together. When we got home our daughter-in-law Jackie was still there—the last of several visitors who had responded to the alarm, including a fire truck.

Needless to say, I am not eager to repeat that embarrassment. So when I found myself sprawled on the floor beside my bed, the alarm button was on my dresser, several feet away. I wasn't worried. I thought I could easily get to my knees and then to my feet. But my right leg is disabled by a stroke and my broken left wrist is in a cast, and the arm is useless. I struggled and struggled but couldn't get up, not even to crawl.

The television was on, but it was a junk program and I couldn't turn it off. I didn't expect my wife home for two or three hours. I couldn't bear the thought of lying on my haunches for two or three hours watching junk TV.

The telephone had been knocked off the table and lay on

the floor in two pieces. I managed to reach it and put it back together and got a dial tone. Salvation.

I hated to do it but I decided to call my son Doug. My granddaughter Adriana answered the phone. Doug wasn't home. I described my plight, emphasizing that I wasn't hurt.

She said, "I'll be right over. I'm leaving right now." She lives in Linda Vista, about 20 minutes away. I lay on the floor like an overturned beetle, awaiting deliverance.

A few minutes later the phone rang. I answered. It was the fire department. The fireman asked me if I was Jack Smith at my address. I said "Yes," and he said, "We'll be there in a few minutes."

I yelled, "Use the back door!" and lay back wondering, "What hath God wrought?"

Several minutes later I heard a commotion at the back door and my granddaughter and three paramedics burst in simultaneously. One of them gave me a hand and raised me to my feet. I thanked him and he said, "We'll just take some Playboys."

He was referring to a column I wrote a month or two ago after the county had barred the magazine from all fire stations. I had a large hoard of old Playboys and offered them to any firemen who applied. I told him where I kept them and said, "Take all you want."

"No thanks," he said. "Just kidding."

It turned out my grandson Chris, recently discharged from the Army and now employed as a security officer, had called 911, which alerted the paramedics. My grandson goes by the book in an emergency.

Jackie soon arrived on the scene, saying she was going to make my dinner. Meanwhile my wife had called and been informed of developments. She said that she was going to pick up something for my dinner, evidently feeling guilty for leaving me alone.

But Jackie was not to be discouraged. She drove down to the market and came back with what she called "beautiful" string beans and broccoli, both of which I hate.

Jackie then went foraging and found a bottle of un-iced champagne in the bar and we agreed that we ought to toast the fact that I was uninjured, even if the champagne was warm.

My wife came home while we were drinking the champagne and we had to give her a glass, which she did not decline.

At least it wasn't as bad as the last time, when I accidentally set off the alarm. On that occasion one of the calls went to the office of my older son, Curt, who was not in. His assistant, not knowing what else to do, looked up Curt's relatives and called the first name. It happened to be a niece of mine who lives out of town. She was panicked but she didn't have the slightest idea what to do.

My wife got home in time to make me a vodka tonic fix. I needed it. She had brought me a dinner of pasta and string beans.

Trading Figure Skating
for Wheelchair Skills

Monday, January 2, 1995

I T   W A S   a banner year for me.

Although I lost some physical skills—for example, I can no longer figure skate nor tie a necktie—I learned how to handle a wheelchair and how to walk with a cane.

Always new horizons.

I believe I experienced some intellectual development, also. I read a book every night after television and relearned many words I had forgotten.

My wife and I saw some wonderful movies: "Casablanca," "For Whom the Bell Tolls" and "The Best Years of Our Lives" among them.

I made several new professional acquaintances—a neurologist, a plastic surgeon, an orthopedist, a podiatrist and an audiologist. The neurologist diagnosed my Parkinson's disease, the dermatologist diagnosed my skin cancer and the plastic surgeon excised it. The orthopedist put a cast on my broken wrist, the podiatrist attended to my broken ankle, the audiologist fitted me with hearing aids.

I also became friends with an athletic young physical therapist named Kathy Doubleday, who comes to my house twice a week to give me a workout. She looks like a college cheerleader.

Also among the new friends I've acquired is Sylvia Carter, who stays with me when my wife is at work and drives me to my various doctors' appointments. Sylvia also fixes my breakfast and sometimes goes out to lunch with me. Sylvia is from Belize. She speaks with a lovely accent and calls me "Zhock." Sometimes in the car, she sings along with the radio.

The reason we have Sylvia is that I am impetuous and my wife is afraid that I will try to walk around the house without assistance and break something else. I have already broken that ankle and the wrist—and I seem to have damaged a rotator cuff in my left shoulder, so that it gives me excruciating pain when I try to put on or take off a shirt. It's the same kind of injury Orel Hershiser had. However, since I'm not a pitcher it doesn't matter that much.

During this year, my relationship with my wife became stronger than ever. Wherever I go, she has to walk on my right side, holding me by the arm. Otherwise, I tend to fall.

She also dresses and undresses me because I can't handle the subtle movements required. Also, I can't button a shirt or get into a coat or tie my shoelaces. It takes about as long to dress me as it must have taken to dress Queen Victoria.

She also takes me to the bathroom. This becomes an embarrassing problem when I have to go in a public place, such as a restaurant. Sometimes she simply commandeers the room until I have finished.

Assisting me when I walk has caused one problem. She says I have a tendency to crowd her off to the right, so that she is always bumping into walls or furniture, and once or twice I almost shoved her into our swimming pool.

Besides escorting me, she has to prepare my pills and insulin shots four times a day. I give the shots to myself, but she has to get them ready. I have a bedside bell that I ring when I need her.

As I've said, this has brought us closer together. Perhaps too close. I sometimes think she resents it when I ring the bell, but she never says anything but, "What is it?"

Sylvia has also been trained to respond to my bell. Sometimes I need her to bring me a Coke or turn a newspaper page. Since breaking my left wrist, I have been unable to turn the pages. It is impossible to do with one hand.

My two daughters-in-law have been wonderful. Gail, the physical therapist, has furnished me with a basket full of marbles that I am supposed to pick up between the thumb and fingers of my hand, now that the cast is off. She has also given me a ball of putty that I am supposed to work in my hand to strengthen the wrist and the fingers.

A couple of days before Christmas, the two of them took me to Bullock's Pasadena to buy a Christmas present for my wife. Before shopping, we had lunch in the tearoom. My French daughter-in-law, Jackie, and I each had a glass of Chardonnay, but my Italian daughter-in-law, Gail, the designated driver, abstained.

We had no sooner started through the store than I saw a

gray-green pantsuit with a mandarin collar. "That's it!" I said at once.

My wife wore it on Christmas night. She looked beautiful. I haven't lost my touch.

I'm a lucky man to have such a family. As for New Year's resolutions, I have only the same old one:

Try to keep on living and see what happens next.

He'd Give Her the Chirp Off His Back

Monday, January 16, 1995

B E I N G rather homebound for the time being, I have become aware of several household phenomena that had previously escaped my notice.

My wife talks to birds.

We have three parakeets and a cockatiel. The cockatiel is smaller than a parrot, but just as mean. Early in the morning, when my wife is preparing to go to work, he sometimes spews out a stream of abuse, strident and unrelenting.

They are not words, understand, just harsh, nerve-racking squawks. After so much of this, my wife says something like, "Oh, be quiet you. I'll get around to you in a minute."

She often commiserates with the bird, saying such things as, "I know. You want to be free. But I can't let you out."

She does not use the silly falsetto that many women affect when talking to infants or the lower species. She speaks in her natural alto, which is a blessing, and she always uses perfect English, as she does in all her conversations. She never stoops to baby talk. How are the animals going to learn perfect English if you use bad grammar?

One morning, while she was giving the bird some philosophical reassurance, I called out to her. "Why do you talk to that bird?"

"Because he sometimes answers me," she said. "He chirps." She added: "You don't chirp."

As a skeptic I don't believe birds can talk, although some species can learn to speak a few words. What they can't do is think, as we do.

You may remember that a few years ago, I had an incident with a cockatiel owned by my wife. He eventually died of meanness. Once when I was home alone, he escaped from his cage and flew down into our deep Jacuzzi bathtub. I got into the bathtub and caught him. He bit me, fixing his beak in a death grip on my thumb. I climbed with difficulty out of the tub, marched across the bathroom and shoved him into his cage, breaking his grip and leaving a bloody wound.

Quite distinctly the bird said, "Big deal." I had never heard him say those words or any words before. I do not know how to account for his contemptuous comment. He never talked to me again.

So I don't think my wife is actually having a conversation with her bird—but evidently, she does.

I know many people swear they talk with their dogs and cats, but I don't believe it. Oh, you can give a dog a simple command such as "Fetch!" and it will fetch whatever it is you throw out. Then the dog will stand there stupidly, wagging its tail, waiting for the next command.

I have noticed my wife has sometimes used her technique with me when she is trying to disabuse me of some heresy, talking in a low-pitched voice and using perfect English. It doesn't work on me because I'm not a dog.

We have to keep our dog tied up because she gets over the fence and neighbors have to bring her home. We don't know how she gets out, but we don't want her running around the neighborhood.

If she could speak English, I would just say to her, "Don't run away and you'll be free to run around the yard to your heart's content." She would have her freedom, and I would have peace of mind.

I know some animals are smart and can do astounding things. But the smartest dog in the world can't parse a sentence. I suspect birds are a lot dumber than dogs and cats, although they can be trained to do simple tricks.

What bothers me is my wife's complaint that I can't even chirp. I probably have many shortcomings as a husband, but not being able to chirp is not one of them.

I know how to chirp. "Chirp. Chirp." See, it's that easy. If I start chirping every time I want something, the next thing you know, I'll be standing at attention every time she says "Fetch."

Even a bird isn't that dumb.

I guess my wife loves birds because they are so beautiful and fragile and because of their lovely song. But what she sees in that curmudgeon cockatiel that grinds out his grating complaint every morning, I can't understand.

Big deal.

Shaving Him From Becoming a Stubble Bum

Monday, January 30, 1995

BEING SEMI-RETIRED, and not obliged to shave every day, I don't.

Consequently, I often look like a bum, or like a man who is

beginning to grow a beard.

There is a fashion among certain types of men for looking unshaven. They often have a two- or three-day growth of beard that gives them a manly, rough-hewn sort of look. This was often affected by Humphrey Bogart and lately by Mel Gibson.

On them, the unshaven look fits an image of the rough-and-ready he-man and evidently is thought attractive by certain types of women.

A beard is, of course, aside from other obvious physiological differences, a phenomenon that sets men and women apart. Men have beards, women do not. Or not usually. The Bearded Lady was a feature of the Barnum & Bailey Circus for decades, though I don't know why she was such an attraction. She certainly had the dullest job imaginable, and one that required no talent whatever. That she was a woman with a beard made her remarkable.

When I don't shave for two or three days, I develop an unsightly growth of gray stubble that does nothing to make me look manly, like Gibson, or sinister, like Bogart. I don't look glamorous. I just look like I need a shave.

The longer one lets a beard grow, the harder it is to get a clean shave. When I look at myself in the mirror, I can't believe that I have been shaving that face for 60 years. I don't even remember how I did it. For years I have been using an electric razor, not as efficient as the old straight edge that I have never used.

Lately, I find the electric razor is not efficient in cutting a two- or three-day growth. The stubble has become too long and too tough. Consequently, I tend to go a day or two more, which makes the problem all the more acute.

Consequently, I have had to go to a barbershop and get a shave—something I had done only once or twice in my life. I had been going to my barber, Rudy, for 15 years or so, but he had never shaved me. The other day when I asked for a shave, he was taken aback. He said he hadn't shaved a customer for at least five years, but he would try. The result was adequate but not prepossessing.

The next time I let it grow even longer. Long curly hairs were growing out of my neck. These either slipped through the teeth of the electric razor or got caught in them and were painfully ripped out.

Then, as my wife and I were driving in Glendale one Saturday, we spotted what appeared to be an Armenian barbershop. I decided to get a shave. It seemed to me an Armenian barber from the old country would know how to give a man an old-fashioned shave.

He did. After a few flourishes of his towel and the application of certain powders and lotions, he set to work with a straight edge. I remembered the story of Napoleon's barber, who held the little colonel's life in his hands. The Armenian barber finished in half an hour, with no accidents. It cost $6.

The next time my beard grew out, I tried shaving it myself. I used one of those throwaway razors my wife had bought for me. They come several in a package, and you discard them after one use. It was a sloppy job—and tedious.

I decided there must be a better way. "Maybe I could shave you," my wife said. She is always volunteering. Well, why not? She did almost everything else for me. Since I broke my wrist, she has learned to button my shirts, tie my neckties and fix my nightly vodka tonic. Why couldn't she shave me now and then?

I lathered my face up for her and she went at it—not with the Armenian flourish, but with a certain French stolidity. It couldn't have been easy. We had no barber's chair. We both had to stand in a cramped space beside the wash basin. When she finished, she said, "*Voila!*" and stepped back to admire her work.

I found she had missed rather large patches of beard and

abraded the skin in two or three places. All in all, though, I looked fairly presentable. When I went out that evening, only a few people said, "What happened to you?"

I'm hoping she'll get better as she has more practice. I may suffer a few wounds now and then, but at least I won't look like a second-rate Mel Gibson.

And it will save me six bucks every time.

His Family Shifts to Second... Jack Into High

Monday, February 13, 1995

W E   H A D a family crisis over the weekend of February 4. My wife drove to Bakersfield to visit an ailing sister. That left me home alone.

I have a problem with my balance. I tend to fall, sometimes with grievous consequences. Although out of the cast now, my left wrist is still too painful for free movement.

My wife insists I not go anywhere alone, with some polite exceptions in the interest of privacy. Even then, I am always to be within calling distance. We remember too well the time I had to be rescued by the fire department when I fell when I was alone.

My caretaker, Sylvia Carter, does not work weekends, but my family volunteered to pitch in, not knowing, I suspect, the problems involved.

But the family was great.

My daughter-in-law Gail, the physical therapist, took the first morning. That was easy. My wife had given me my breakfast blood test, insulin shot and pills before she left.

Gail had a client in the afternoon, so my son Curt took

over. Gail had instructed him to see that I got some exercise—perhaps a walk around the patio—but he busied himself with my computer and spent the entire afternoon moving hundreds of my columns from floppy disks to the hard disk. Meanwhile I napped, mostly.

In the late afternoon my son Doug took over. Curt doesn't like needles and the sight of blood, so Doug gave me my dinner blood test.

In this procedure you are required to get a drop of blood on the end of a finger by pricking it with a needle. Then the drop of blood is transferred to a sensitized strip, which is placed in a meter that gives the blood-sugar level. Doug let the first drop of blood get away and had to massage my forearm and hand to get another one. I dropped it on the strip and the reading was normal.

Meanwhile, my daughter-in-law Jackie, Doug's wife, came with a dinner she had prepared at home. Pork chops and green beans. Before serving dinner, she asked if I would like my usual fix. I said indeed I would.

Every evening before dinner my wife mixes us a vodka tonic. Unless we are out at a party, it is the only thing we drink. Jackie is familiar with wines, but evidently she had no experience with mixed drinks.

"Here you are, Mr. Smith," she said, placing the drink on a table by my chair. I picked it up gratefully and took a sip. It numbed my tongue. It was at least half vodka. I had tried to get my wife to increase the vodka, but she had refused.

"How is your drink, Mr. Smith?" Jackie asked.

"Oh, fine. Fine," I said, not wanting her to take it back.

Curt stayed for dinner, and we had a fine dinner conversation, enlivened, I may say, by my own input. I seemed to be unusually garrulous.

After dinner Doug treated my big toe. That is an affliction

I don't believe I have mentioned in my catalogue of woes. It is what the doctor calls an ulcer. It was about the size of a quarter and was apparently not healing when I went to the podiatrist. He said it was a good thing I had come in. Diabetics, he said, often have sores that won't heal, especially on their feet, and these can turn into gangrene, which might require amputation. With no big toe, I realized, I would have no balance whatever.

The doctor told me to soak the toe twice a day for 20 minutes in a tub of medicated water, then bandage it with gauze. I have been doing that for two weeks, and the ulcer has grown smaller.

But the doctor also told me to rub the toe vigorously to increase the circulation. The first night Sylvia rubbed it vigorously indeed. That night I had shooting pains in the toe that kept me awake until dawn.

Doug did a fine job on my toe, but the bandage he wrapped it in looked like a turban.

I must say it isn't as bad as it could be, however. The other day my skin man noticed some flaking on my face. He checked my record and found I had had bypass surgery several years ago. He said he wanted me to take a blood test to see whether the transfusions then had given me HIV.

I had once joked with a doctor that I had everything but AIDS, and he had said, "Don't be too sure."

Fortunately, the test proved negative.

I drank Jackie's fix at dinner and enjoyed every drop.

Oddly, though, I don't remember going to bed.

After All These Years He's Now a Ladies' Man

Monday, July 3, 1995

IN MY LATER YEARS my life has become dominated by women. It's a fate that seems to overtake many men, but somehow I escaped in childhood. Neither my mother nor my older sister had much influence over me.

I was a man's man, or thought I was. Even in my marriage, which has lasted 56 years, I remained free of female domination. Not that my wife isn't a woman of strong will. But she is not overbearing.

Suddenly I find myself in the hands of women who are not relatives, either by blood or marriage. They simply seem to be in control of some phases of my life, whether I like it or not.

One is a young woman I call my keeper. Her name is Eleanor Yvonne Gabourel.

People call her Elly, though I rather favor Yvonne. Elly is from Belize.

She stays with me at home four days a week while my wife is at work. She prepares my breakfast and lunch, launders my shirts and underwear, does light housekeeping and fetches for me.

She also drives me to my doctor appointments. She is a good driver. She never makes left turns in front of oncoming traffic. She is patient. She does not have a heavy foot, like my wife.

She is pretty, petite and smart. She is married to a man from Belize and has a 9-year-old daughter. She laughs easily. Altogether she is a very good keeper.

My physical therapist is a young woman named Kathy

Doubleday. She is very lithe and athletic. She works with me two days a week, making me walk without my cane or walker. When my women are not with me, I am dependent on such props.

My third woman is Christine Steffanus, my gym instructor at the Pasadena Athletic Club. I call her "Cookie." I don't know why. She isn't especially sweet. She doesn't crumble. But I think it suits her.

She is a hard taskmaster. She makes me walk without my cane, urging me to take long steps with my lame right leg. She is unrelenting. "Take long steps," she commands. "Put that right foot out!" She is impervious to my complaints.

She is planning to get married next year, as soon as she and her fiance save enough money for the wedding. I urged her not to wait. You don't have to have a big wedding. Besides, I thought that being married might soften her attitude toward me.

My wife likes these women. She is always asking me, "How did you get along with Kathy today?" Or with Elly or Cookie. I think she sympathizes with them, and she feels that they are relieving her of some of the burden.

The other woman I have to live with, of course, is my wife. She is incredibly strong. She complained over the weekend that I was depressed, and she didn't need that.

Though I have plenty of reason, I try not to be depressed. Depression is merely a form of self-pity. My wife is hard to depress, but sometimes I'm too much for her.

My wife runs my life. She allows me one beer a day. Every day about 4 o'clock, Elly opens a bottle of beer and sets it on my table, or desk if I'm working. I suppose she'd get me another one if I insisted, but she'd have to tell my wife and it wouldn't be worth the hassle.

"Elly tells me you had two bottles of beer today. How come?"

"Because I wanted two."

That should be the end of it, but of course I'd feel guilty.

Every evening before dinner my wife makes a vodka tonic for both of us. We call it our fix. I don't get two, except when we go out to dinner I sometimes manage to get two—sometimes even two and a glass of wine. Or two.

On those occasions, however, I find it harder than usual to walk. My wife has to hold onto my right arm and sometimes I run her off the sidewalk or into a wall.

These restraints naturally annoy me. I have been a free spirit all my life. I don't feel that I need anyone's permission to do anything legal. On the other hand, if my wife were to desert me or turn on me I'd be helpless. If she deserted me so would Elly, Kathy and Cookie.

Then, of course, I could have all the beer I wanted and all the vodka. But that would turn me into a sot, offensive not only to myself but also to everyone else.

I am too lucky to be depressed. I have a wonderful family, including those other two women in my life, my daughters-in-law. I have my books; I have my dogs.

On the other hand, I don't see why I can't have two beers.

He Will Never Forget Old What's His Name

Monday, November 20, 1995

HAVING BEEN subjected to several in the past few years, I have become wary of various hospital procedures, all of which, I am assured, are necessary for my continued good health. Or rather, to forestall my immediate demise.

About two years ago, in Huntington Memorial Hospital, I endured, though badly, a test called Magnetic Resonance Imaging, or MRI.

I really didn't know what its purpose was or how it worked. I was stretched out on a hospital bed, as I remember, and subjected to a series of dreadful noises.

I was in rather unstable condition at the time, having recently suffered a heart attack and a stroke that crippled my right leg, and I did not endure the MRI very well.

After I'd heard enough of the cataclysmic noises, I finally rebelled. "Take me out of here!" I yelled at the technician. The doctor called my wife, who was waiting elsewhere in the hospital, and asked her to see if she could calm me down. "We're almost finished," he assured her.

She came to my side and urged me to cooperate, which I did. When the test was completed, the doctor said it showed that I had had a stroke, which I already knew.

Recently my neurologist was testing my reflexes (which weren't too bad) and asked me if I had noticed any memory loss.

Well, who hasn't?

Only a day or two earlier, while waiting for my wife to come home from work, I was watching an old movie starring Burt Reynolds, Christopher Reeve and Kathleen Turner. Although I knew them all quite well, I couldn't remember any of their names. When my wife came home, she asked me who was in the movie. I couldn't tell her. I said, "Oh, you know." She watched it a few minutes and then said, "That's Kathleen Turner. And that's Christopher Reeve and that, of course, is Burt Reynolds." Of course.

The doctor told me I might have had a couple of minor strokes, and he said he wanted me to take an MRI. "Not again!" I protested. Of course I had to do it. I confessed to the doctor about my previous bad experience with an MRI, but he assured me there was nothing to it.

My wife drove me to the MRI lab near the hospital. The technologist was very reassuring. He had me lie on a padded bed and I was automatically enclosed, except that I could see through a small window.

My wife's face appeared in the window, smiling reassuringly. The test began. First it was the sustained sound of a jackhammer. It lasted three minutes, my wife informed me.

My wife told me over some sort of intercom that the next test would be only two minutes. Evidently she was in touch with the technologist, who was using her to keep me tractable.

The next sound I heard was that of an automobile starter. It was trying hard, but it wasn't starting the car. This is a maddening sound. You keep praying for the car to start.

The next sound (3½ minutes) was some kind of machinery. My wife told me it sounded like an old washing machine. It was endurable.

It was followed by a series of loud noises reminiscent of factories. Thank God there were no explosions.

Finally it was over. I had borne up quite well.

I asked the technician, "How can you tell anything about my brain from all that?"

He took us into a room where a panel of images was on the wall. Evidently they were pictures of my brain reacting to all those noises. My doctor would study those pictures, he said, and diagnose my problems.

I left the laboratory still skeptical that any trustworthy diagnosis could come from such a procedure. Nevertheless, I was proud I had endured the test without cracking up.

We stopped at a Shaker for breakfast after the test. My wife told me to order the waffle combo for her, and left for the ladies room. When the waitress came I couldn't remember what my wife had ordered.

During breakfast I kept trying to remember what MRI stood for. "Magnetic Resonance Imaging," she told me.

It sounded like gobbledygook to me.

I didn't mention it to my wife, but on the way home I realized I had forgotten the names of the three stars in whatever the name of that movie was. The only name I could remember was Christopher Isherwood. Instead of banging your ears with loud noises, it seemed to me that they could learn a lot more about your brain by playing old movies and asking you to identify the players.

Actually, from those images on the wall I didn't see anything wrong with my brain, except that it was smaller than I had imagined.

Family Pools Resources to Celebrate His Birthday

Monday, September 4, 1995

I CELEBRATED another birthday on a recent Sunday. I say I celebrated it. I simply had it. My family celebrated it.

I had invited them over for a swimming party, it being insufferably hot. They came en masse. They had to be fed. My wife drove down to the market and came back with chicken, Italian sausage, soft drinks and beer.

My grandson Casey, 16, cooked the meat on our barbecue. Someone had brought a gooey cake. A few brought presents, though they know there's nothing I need, except love and compassion.

Speaking of compassion, my wife let me have two vodka

tonics, instead of my usual one; I also had three glasses of wine and a bottle of beer. All of which put me in a celebratory mood.

I got one card from my oldest son, Curt, his wife, Gail, and their three children, Alison, Casey and Trevor. (Alison was absent, having gone off to Cornell University, in Ithaca, N.Y.) It was a fold-over card, with a message on the front and a zinger on the third page.

"We can tell each other our most sincere, profound thoughts. Why?

"We're family!

"We can get together after a long time apart and still have a good time! Why?

"We're family!

"We can make fun of you on your birthday and abuse you and knock you. Why?"

And finally, on the last page, the abuse:

"You're old!"

Though I was perfectly aware of my advanced years, it was rather a downer to have that fact pointed out by my loved ones.

I had never thought of myself as old. I was the perennial juvenile. I thought of myself as Maurice Chevalier, in "Gigi," when he asks Hermione Gingold, "Am I growing old?" and she says, "Oh, no, not you."

I had worn my swimming trunks, but did not go in the pool. That was for the kids. My other granddaughter, Adriana, was there, an elegantly tall young woman, and her older brother Chris, muscled and self-confident after two years in the Army.

Their parents, my younger son Doug and my daughter-in-law, Jackie, were present and helped put away the wine. Also present were my wife's niece and nephew, Jean and Mike O'Neill, from Bakersfield. (Mike and Jean had recently vacationed in France with Doug and Jackie.)

266

Casey did not swim. He said he was too sore from the first week of football practice at Brentwood. His younger brother, Trevor, swam like a seal.

Doug did not swim. He said he had never liked swimming. I was shocked. We had taken him and Curt to Brookside Park for swimming lessons when they were small boys. Both had learned to swim, and Curt had won a lifeguard certificate. I thought they had loved it.

"I was always cold," Doug said. "I never liked it. I never swim in our pool at home."

I realized, sadly, that you never know whether you're pleasing your children or not. I had to console myself with the thought that at least we had taught the boys how to swim, an absolute necessity for kids in Southern California, where there are so many pools.

The only non-family guests were Kathy Doubleday, my physical therapist, and her fiance, Ron Hess, an engineering student at UCLA. Kathy is a neighbor and takes me swimming in the pool one or two days a week. One of the disadvantages of being old is that I can't get into the pool by myself, having had a disabling stroke a year or so ago. I know the word is politically incorrect, but I'm handicapped. I think we should call things by their names.

I have a card that permits me to use disabled parking. I'm told that parking in a disabled space without a card can get you a $1,000 fine. My wife doesn't like to leave me alone in the car when she gets out to go shopping because I am not a driver and have no right to use the card. I point out that I am handicapped and I am in the car. I don't believe any officer would give me a ticket.

I suppose that's the sort of thing husbands and wives argue about when they get old. My wife, however, is not old. I don't know how she managed to escape old age when I was drifting into it so helplessly. She just doesn't seem to have the genes for it.

She's forever young.

Being old, I suppose I ought to review my lifestyle and find a better way to deal with it. I think I will stick with a life plan that I decided on several years ago and reaffirmed recently.

I think I'll just try to stay alive and see what happens next.

White Goose Sighted but Doesn't Make the List

Monday, December 18, 1995

ONCE AGAIN my wife and I were invited to attend the Jack and Denny Smith Bird Walk at Descanso Gardens and, on a recent Sunday morning, we went. The invitation came from Karen Johnson, first vice president of the San Fernando Valley Audubon Society and indefatigable leader of the walk.

The Society's publication, Phainopepla, graciously noted that the walk has been held for several years to honor me for my "unprecedented sighting of a common grackle at the Smith residence on Mt. Washington (the Smiths were the recipients of San Fernando Valley's Special Award in 1993)."

Though I have never actively sought recognition for my sighting, which has been the object of much skepticism by ornithologists and common birders, it was gratifying to see my coup acknowledged by such a prestigious publication.

It was a beautiful day at Descanso Gardens. The bird walk started at 8 o'clock with about 30 of us in attendance. Johnson welcomed us and introduced my wife and me. For the first time, I went in a wheelchair, with my wife pushing.

As usual, the walk began with numerous sightings. Johnson noted a flock of yellow-rumped warblers. As often happens to me on bird walks, I didn't see them. Someone also reported seeing a flock of acorn woodpeckers that also escaped my notice. "See them moving frantically from place to place," Johnson called out. "They're eating insects."

I don't know whether my eyesight is deteriorating or whether I just happened to be looking at the wrong place at the wrong time, but I missed several of the sightings that later turned up on our list. Perhaps I was distracted by looking for another grackle.

"There's a hummingbird hovering at 12 o'clock," Johnson said. But I didn't know whether she meant 12 o'clock high or 12 o'clock low, and I missed it.

Later she identified a "flock of about 200 cedar waxwings." It was cedar waxwings, my wife reminded me, that used to get drunk off the nectar of a cotoneaster bush near a corner of our house. They used to really get soused and flop around drunkenly. It was delightful. Somehow a drunken bird is not disgusting.

"Whatever happened to them?" I asked my wife.

"We cut down the cotoneaster when we remodeled. To build your office. Remember?"

All things considered, I don't think the trade was worth it.

We soon came to the pond. For years this has been a refuge for many water birds, including the resident great blue heron. Sure enough Johnson cried out, "There he is! The great blue heron! He's perching on that branch."

I looked in vain for the great blue heron, which I had seen in previous years. But I did see a remarkable bird—a long-necked swanlike creature with a red beak. It sailed about majestically.

"That's the Australian black swan," Johnson said, and I felt better about having missed the great blue heron.

A moment later Johnson identified another remarkable bird—the green heron, not as big as the great blue heron but greener.

I identified a bird that I thought might be the great blue heron, but Johnson said "It's not blue, it's white. It's a goose."

Which is what I felt like.

The gardens were lush with greenery. Sycamores, live oaks, pines. A ginkgo spread an umbrella of yellow leaves and laid a carpet of them on the ground.

At one point the trail was rather steep, and I could tell my wife was winded. "Can I help?" said a male voice with a heavy British accent. He was a lean young man with a large walrus mustache. He took the wheelchair and pushed me up the hill. He said he was a Yorkshireman, name of Alan Dunn.

We came finally to the "counting bridge," which is where we stop to list all the birds we have seen. The birders began calling out the names and Johnson checked them off on a list.

It was a remarkable count. Wood duck, mallard, ring-necked duck, American coot, California gull, mourning dove, white-throated swift, Anna's hummingbird, Allen's hummingbird, belted kingfisher, acorn woodpecker, Nutall's woodpecker, northern flicker, black phoebe, scrub jay, American crow, common raven, plain titmouse, bushtit, Bewick's wren, ruby-crowned kinglet, hermit thrush, American robin, wrentit, northern mockingbird, California thrasher, cedar waxwing.

I wonder why there were so many birds on the list that I didn't see. As I said, maybe it was because I was concentrating so hard on the grackle. I wonder also whether I might hope that in time the bird would come to be known as Smith's grackle. It makes as much sense as Anna's hummingbird and Nutall's woodpecker.

After all "common" grackle is much too common for a bird that scarce.

CHAPTER 13

What It's All About

Peanut Butter, Eggs on His
Stay-Healthy List

Thursday, February 28, 1991

A READER named Sava William Jacobson, of Sherman Oaks, writes to ask if I will divulge my secrets for remaining healthy.

I would be happy to share my secrets, but I'm not sure my readers in general have the discipline to follow my advice.

"I recall that some years ago you had a bypass operation," Jacobson says, "and that thereafter you went on a strict diet and exercise regimen."

That isn't quite what happened. I did have a bypass, but I did not immediately begin regular exercise, and my diet was rather self-indulgent. I have always liked hot dogs, bacon, eggs and peanut butter, and I saw no reason for living many more years if I were deprived of them.

I convinced my cardiologist that I was getting enough exercise by walking up and down malls while shopping. He was skeptical, but they don't like to tell you what to do.

Then one day a friend and I walked up a long flight of stairs together. When we reached the top I was puffing laboriously. My friend was worried. He had had a bypass a few years before me, and he said, "You'd better shape up, man."

I enrolled in the Huntington Hospital cardiac rehabilitation program. Three mornings a week I worked out with other patients under the direction of three frisky young women who frolicked with us and played improbable medleys on the stereo while we exercised.

At the end of three months I was discharged and was

declared the "most improved" member of the group.

I then enrolled in Ray Steffanus' class at the Pasadena Athletic Club. Three mornings a week I exercised under Ray's direction, riding a bicycle, lifting light dumbbells, using a leg lift and working various light arm machines.

I have been doing that ever since.

However, I will use almost any excuse to avoid getting up early and going to the class. On an average, I miss at least once a week.

However, one incentive for going is that after the workouts I indulge myself in a breakfast at the Konditori, Rose City or some other Pasadena cafe. Having earned this modest pleasure by exercising, I usually have pancakes, bacon and eggs. (Sometimes champagne and orange juice.)

Since my wife works, I have to fix my own lunch, or eat down the hill at the Packard Grill, where I usually have an Italian sausage salad or a hamburger. At home I heat a small can of chili or pasta in the microwave and eat it with a diet Pepsi.

For dinner I'm at the mercy of the draw—the draw being whatever microwave dinner my wife happens to pull out of the cupboard. Usually these are chicken and pasta dishes, but sometimes we get cheese enchiladas or lasagna.

I almost never eat dessert, but every night before going to bed I eat a dish of frozen yogurt. My favorite is chocolate chip.

Meanwhile, the friend who cautioned me at the top of the stairs has had a *second* bypass. Evidently they're only good for eight or 10 years.

If that's true, my time will soon be up. I don't know whether I want to go through the ordeal of another bypass. On the other hand I do enjoy bacon and eggs and frozen yogurt and various other amenities, including watching sex and violence on television with my wife, so I'll probably be willing to go through with the operation to gain a few more years.

When you find yourself in my predicament, you find out things about yourself. For example, there are certain things I won't do, even to add a few years to my life. My wife bought me an exercise bicycle, but I never used it. I said it was too boring. She bought me a television set to put in the bedroom so I could watch television while cycling. I tried it once or twice.

Eventually I gave the bicycle to my older son. He put it in his bedroom but never used it. His wife finally made him get rid of it. My younger son's wife took it and put it in her bedroom, but never used it. I have no idea where it is today.

My regimen seems to be working. I usually ache in the morning and get tired in the afternoon, but who doesn't? My weight has been stable for years. I can still wear all my old clothes.

Undoubtedly, the most important health measure I have ever taken was to quit smoking. That is why I am alive today and able to eat bacon and eggs and hot dogs and hamburgers and chocolate chip yogurt.

If I have to have another bypass, I probably will. I have unfinished business. Among other projects I have just started to read the King James version of the Bible, top to bottom.

Surely God won't let me die until I finish that, no matter how many hot dogs I eat.

Count on It: It Is Seven Years to Millennium

Monday, January 10, 1994

M Y   O L D   F R I E N D John Weaver called me the morning of December 31 to ask if I had seen a story on Page 1 of The

Times that day about New Year's Eve parties.

I had. It noted that "the granddaddy of all New Year's is fast approaching. The turn of the millennium: 1999 is six years away."

Weaver knew I had often argued that the millennium would turn at the end of the year 2000, not 1999.

"I thought you might get a column out of it," he said.

I told him I doubted it. I had already written two or three columns on the subject without damaging the misguided popular notion that centuries expire with years ending in 99.

I have a six-inch file of letters, most of them either angry or patronizing, explaining, often at great length, why I am wrong. Some of them are accompanied by long mathematical tables allegedly proving their theses.

I have been called all kinds of names, from irreverent to merely stupid, and some die-hards have even promised to pray for me.

What amazes me is that otherwise intelligent and erudite people cling to the notion that the 20th Century will end on December 31, 1999. In fact, it will end on December 31, 2000.

What surprised me was the academic credentials and the vehemence of some who disagreed. After a heated exchange of letters, a UCLA professor abandoned the argument, implying that I had insulted his intelligence. A retired Caltech professor reluctantly conceded that I was right.

Quoting the Millennium Society, the Times story acknowledged that some people hold my point of view, but our arguments were dismissed as "technical" and we were characterized as "smarty-pants."

There is really nothing to it. There was no year 0. The first year of the Christian Era was AD 1. The first decade ended at the end of AD 10. The first century ended at the end of AD 100. The 20th Century will end on December 31, 2000, and the 21st Century will begin the next day—January 1, 2001.

It is incredible how frenzied the arguments against this simple logic can be.

Readers' arguments include treatises on the origin of the Gregorian calendar, the historicity of the birth of Jesus and tables of exhaustive calculations.

None of these alleged proofs mean a thing. The simple fact is that the final dates of decades and centuries end in 0. The dates of new decades and centuries end in 1.

In my losing campaign to establish this fact, I have quoted at least a dozen prestigious encyclopedias, almanacs, scientific institutions and pundits, including the late Isaac Asimov, the century's most popular science writer.

Writing 10 years ago, Asimov tried to enlighten his readers: "And the 10th and last decade of the 20th Century will begin on January 1, 1991, not a moment sooner."

But being wise as well as intelligent, Asimov conceded that the facts would not keep people from celebrating on January 1, 1990. "And 10 years after that," he predicted, "January 1, 2000, will arrive and the whole world will burst with joy. It will be 'a new millennium.' The celebrations will be unbelievable.... But just the same the new millennium will not begin till January 1, 2001."

Although I may not be here, I have no doubt that the whole world will prematurely burst with joy in celebrating the supposed advent of the 21st Century on January 1, 2000.

I can hardly blame them. Who wouldn't want to get out of this wretched century a year early?

Musing over the question in Smithsonian magazine, Chalmers M. Roberts suggests that the popular notion that centuries and millennia begin with a zero at the right end of the year is emotional, not rational, and nothing can be done about it.

"My point," he says, "is that mathematics can't bend a sense of fate, as witness the millenarians who predicted the end of the world as we knew it near the year 1000 and will no doubt do so again as December 31, 1999, and January 1, 2000, approach.

"Meanwhile our hearts will tell us that as soon as we hit that Big Two—2000—a humongous turn will have been made, and then and there we are into the new century."

As I falsely promised when I last mentioned this subject, I am through with it. I rest my case. As Asimov and Roberts suggest, it's emotional, anyway; it's in the heart, not the head. The change from 99 to 00 is somehow transcendental.

I just hope that, in my memory, The Times will have a little front page box on January 1, 2000, saying "No folks, as Jack Smith kept telling us (God rest his soul) today is not the first day of the 21st Century. It won't be for a year yet."

Well, Here We Are
but Who Can Say Why?

Monday, September 26, 1994

I WAS SITTING the other day in Bullock's Pasadena while my wife shopped for a wedding present. I was in a room that seemed to be filled with objets d'art, such as porcelain figurines. I was thinking of nothing in particular, just waiting for my wife and watching other shoppers.

I was seated at a desk on which I saw a small gold case filled with note paper. On the top sheet was written, in ink, the word *Why?* Nothing else.

As I sat there contemplating the anonymous "Why?" I

began to wonder why whoever had written it had done so. Evidently the author was a person, presumably a woman, who, like the rest of us, had no real answer to that question.

Perhaps she had been waiting for someone else, too, and felt, as I did, rather desolate and abandoned. The question, of course, goes back to first things. Why are we here?

As I think I mentioned here recently, the brilliant British physicist Stephen Hawking says in his book "Black Holes and Baby Universes" that he too is searching for the answer.

"Since 1974," he says, "I have been working on combining general relativity and quantum mechanics into a consistent theory. One result of that has been a proposal made in 1983 with Jim Hattle of the University of California at Santa Barbara: that both time and space are finite in extent, but they don't have any boundary or edge. They would be like the surface of the Earth, but with two more dimensions. The Earth's surface is finite in area, but it doesn't have any boundary. In all my travels, I have not managed to fall off the edge of the world. If this proposal is correct, there would be no singularities, and the laws of science would hold everywhere, including at the beginning of the universe. The way the universe would begin could be determined by the laws of science. I would have succeeded in my ambition to discover *how* the universe began.

But I still don't know *why* it began."

That suggests to me that my guess as to why we are here is as good as his, though I know nothing of quantum mechanics and can't even get my VCR-Plus to work.

The question was raised plaintively in that refrain of some years ago: "What's it all about, Alfie?"

Those among us who believe in God have no problem. God created us for reasons of his own. But I keep wondering why, if God is infallible, did we turn out so bad? Assuming that he created us for his own entertainment, he must find watching us much like we find watching sex and violence on television. Surely he could have found some better way for us to procreate than by sexual union. Why did he create two sexes to begin with? Surely he could have foreseen the problems that would cause.

In the evolutionist view, we simply began as one-celled creatures who developed over the millennia into monkeys and then into human beings. That still leaves the question: Why?

Einstein once said, "I shall never believe that God plays dice with the world."

I don't understand what Einstein meant by that any more than I understand his fourth dimension. But it suggests that he believed in God, and that God was responsible for us. That still doesn't answer the question of why?

(As I was sitting there in Bullock's, several young women strolled by. Some had toddlers at their sides or in strollers. It was a Friday. Why weren't these young women working at their jobs while their children were in day-care centers? Isn't that the way it is?)

I'm not a physicist, but I'm entitled to my own theory. I think we have evolved from one-celled creatures, but I think that somewhere along the line something went wrong. Perhaps the creator erred in giving us two sexes and letting us choose our mates. Obviously we have made a lot of other bad choices, and the result is war, crime and what's happened to baseball.

As for why we're here, I think Hawking and his colleagues will discover some day that we're here because there's nowhere else to be.

We might go to the end of the Earth looking for somewhere else to live, but of course, as Hawking points out, the Earth has no end. One good thing about the Earth being round is that you can't fall off.

My wife finally came back for me. She was empty-handed. She had been unable to find a proper present. "What have you been doing?" she asked.

"Oh, thinking," I said.

"What about?" she said.

"Oh," I said, "nothing."

What's it all about, Alfie?

Betting His Stake on the God of Chance

March 9, 1989 and July 2, 1990

WHILE WALKING along our beach in Baja California some years ago, I suddenly realized that God's name was Random Chance.

I duly reported that revelation in this space, and over the years it has inspired unceasing correspondence, pro and con.

Several readers have pointed out that this is probably a misinterpretation of Darwin's theory of evolution, and is outmoded by modern scientific thought.

I feel obliged to say how I came about that notion. It was a flash of intuition. Scientists say human life is far too complex to have evolved by random chance, though chance certainly played a part in it. As several readers have pointed out, Richard Dawkins, in "The Blind Watchmaker," holds that the universe evolved, without design, by what he calls "cumulative selection." Stephen Jay Gould, in "Wonderful Life," calls this force "contingency," observing that A became B and B became C and C became D, and so on, each stage being contingent on the last. Both hold that blind chance could not have produced life.

But both deny that there was any design, any purpose, or any watchmaker.

I hate to give up the name Random Chance, which has served me very well, but one must adjust one's beliefs to the new theories of the scientists. It just won't do to say "Contingency Chance," or "Cumulative Selection." I liked Random Chance because it sounded like a river-boat gambler.

Meanwhile, J. David Archibald, professor of biology at San Diego State University, chides me for saying that "life is the product of random chance, but that cannot be proved, and some scientists deny it."

Prof. Archibald points out that science can prove nothing: "There are differing views on how science progresses, but one common precept is that science cannot prove anything to be true. Rather, it proposes theories that have the potential of being falsified, though totally falsifying a theory is not even possible."

Does that mean that if I say God's name is Random Chance they can't prove it isn't true?

Prof. Archibald says no: "Even though we have far more questions than answers about the origin of life, we do know with as much certainty as one has in science that the combination of elements and molecules to form early life was far from being a totally random process."

Thayer Smith writes again to say that in summarizing the calculations of Boyd Benson, professor of mathematics at Rio Hondo Community College, I did not grasp the magnitude of Prof. Benson's conclusion. The question was, how long would it take a billion monkeys to correctly type the first paragraph of Dickens' "A Tale of Two Cities."

Smith suggests that I was "daunted" by the figures and backed off from quoting them, merely noting Prof. Benson's monumental understatement that it would take "too long to be considered."

Actually, I *was* daunted. I talked to Prof. Benson on the telephone, and although he verified what I took to be his conclusions, I could not believe them. Smith reminds me that the figure was 15 billion (the age of the universe) times 6 followed by 888 zeros. Smith typed out the zeros, which took two-thirds of a page.

Dawkins sets a simpler task for a baby, a monkey or a random computer: typing, at random, the phrase "Methinks it is like a weasel." He says it would take about a million million million million million years. However, he says, if a computer is programmed to examine each letter and choose those that most resemble the target phrase, the results are rather faster. He programmed a computer that did it in 11 seconds. That is the difference between random chance and cumulative selection.

Jim Karugg and Bill Stewart each sent me a copy of "Inflexible Logic," a short story by Russell Maloney in which a wealthy dilettante named Bainbridge sets six chimpanzees at work on typewriters in his conservatory. At once they begin typing out such classics as Trevelyan's "Life of Macaulay," the Confessions of St. Augustine, "Vanity Fair" and the Essays of Montaigne—letter perfect, page after page. A scientist, Prof. Mallard, is so deranged by this astounding feat that he arrives armed one day and shoots all the monkeys to death. He and Bainbridge then kill each other.

Perhaps I should take a lesson from that story and quit fooling around with things I don't understand.

On the other hand, who knows when I might be hit by another flash of intuition?

Perfect Gift for the Man
Who Wants Nothing

Tuesday, December 27, 1977

I AM ONE of those difficult husbands for whom it is almost impossible to buy a successful Christmas present. It isn't that there is nothing I don't already have; it's just that there are so many things I don't want.

So I was not only gratified but quite surprised on Christmas morning when I walked into my den and saw my present. It was not wrapped, but had been set out—assembled, so to speak—so that I would get the full impact of it the instant I entered the room.

My wife and I had exchanged presents with our family on Christmas Eve, but saved our presents to each other for Christmas morning, as our sons and daughters-in-law were doing in their own homes. But I had forgotten the plan, and I made my coffee and sat down with the paper in my usual absent-minded cloud to read the football news.

So, when at last I walked into the den, it took me a moment to comprehend that the articles laid out on my couch were a Christmas present. And then I began to wonder at the memory, understanding and resourcefulness that must have gone into the selection and preparation of that gift.

It would have to have been two or three years earlier that the idea had been planted in her mind, though at the time she couldn't have thought of working it out this way. We had been spending a weekend at our house in Baja and were reading by our Coleman lanterns one night when I came across a quotation I had never heard before—one that struck me as remarkably profound. I read it to her, wanting to share my discovery, but though she appeared to be listening, looking up from her own book, I had no idea that she would ever think of it again.

It was a line from some ancient Roman poet, one whose name I didn't know, which of course didn't necessarily make him obscure. I must remember it, I told myself. I wanted to search out the whole poem, find out exactly what the poet meant.

Often, when I come across something I want to remember I mark the page or make a note on a slip of paper, but more often I foolishly convince myself that I can remember it without props. Then in a day or two I not only can't remember the source, but can't remember the thing to be remembered itself, having only a vague idea that there was something I wanted to remember.

But I remembered that quotation. I thought of it many times. Perhaps I had recalled it out loud once or twice, refreshing my wife's memory of it. But I couldn't remember where I'd read it. I looked in half a dozen books, thinking it would turn up, but it remained elusive. We have stacks of books and magazines in the Baja house already, and I have been through most of them. To this day I have not found the book with that quotation; I don't remember the name of the poet, and I have never encountered anyone among my more erudite friends who ever heard the quotation before.

And there it was, on Christmas morning, laid out in 18 pieces of wooden type—each piece three-quarters of an inch thick and one inch tall, and backwards, of course—the words being in reverse order and each letter backwards, in the way of moveable type. The type face still bore the stain of the ink used to print out the message on a long piece of coarse linen which was also laid out on the couch. There it was—the line from my forgotten Latin poet:

SPEND ALL YOUR KISSES

I plan to fix the wooden letters to my wall, so that I can be reminded every day of their message. It won't bother me that it's backwards. Any pre-electronic newspaperman who still remembers the first time he ever saw his byline on a Linotype slug can read backwards without much trouble.

Until I find the source again and am able to read the poem in full, I may never be sure what the poet meant by that admonition—"Spend all your kisses." It may have been purely a sensuous thought. Poets are not unknown to spend all their kisses. I imagine Lord Byron had a few left when he died of a fever in Greece at the age of 36.

But perhaps it means that there is no point in taking any of one's wealth into the next world. Why keep a kiss, a gesture, a word that might give a moment's pleasure or reassurance to someone else? Years ago I made my first trip to Europe on a reportorial assignment, adequately financed by my newspaper. Despite the temptations of Naples, Rome, Morocco and Athens, I returned with more than $200 in company funds, which I of course returned. Now, as I imagine what I denied myself by not spending that $200, I suspect that I have been too conservative with all my riches.

There is little chance that I will get out of this world with much money; if I should, I expect my heirs to rectify that oversight.

And now—thanks to my wife, to an ancient poet, and to my ability to read backwards—I am not likely to get out with any unspent kisses, either.

Money you can't take with you. Kisses you can't leave behind.